Asahel Stone

Fountain Park Cemetery

Asahel Stone

Fountain Park Cemetery

ISBN/EAN: 9783742825230

Manufactured in Europe, USA, Canada, Australia, Japa

Cover: Foto ©ninafisch / pixelio.de

Manufactured and distributed by brebook publishing software (www.brebook.com)

Asahel Stone

Fountain Park Cemetery

INTRODUCTORY.

It is a recognized fact that all men should be interested in securing a suitable resting place for the departed. Because, from every marble shaft and every velvet mound that rises in the quiet "cities of the dead," a whisper trembles, telling the dreadful finality of human life.

As a matter of history it is well known that many of the best cemeteries in this and other States have been established with great difficulty, and bonded debts and mortgages have been peculiar to their commencement. To plan and establish a cemetery, in harmony with the rigid requirements of the public, is a matter of considerable magnitude. In enterprises of this character the opinions of good citizens are various and as wide apart as the poles, but when success is assured, time soon harmonizes discordant elements. Financial embarrassment is as distressing and hurtful to cemetery corporations as to individuals, and the citizens of this vicinity are congratulated, not only upon the happy culmination of their long deferred hopes, but also upon being relieved from any burden of debt, by the broad benevolence and comprehensive charity of the donor of Fountain Park Cemetery.

This park and cemetery are valuable acquisitions to Randolph county. A park, to be touched and re-touched, by the hand of art, until it teems and glows with oriental grandeur, cannot be too highly appreciated. A burial place, to be so peerless and beautiful, dedicated in love, sanctified by the prayers of the people, baptized in the smiles of heaven, is an offering worthy of acceptation. Hence, in the light of existing facts, it is meet, proper, and in accordance with propriety, that all citizens should co-operate cheerfully and zealously with the management of the cemetery and park.

It is obvious to thoughtful men that a neglected cemetery, or one undesirable for burying purposes, is a disgrace to any community; and that a high civilization demands something better than the crude simplicity of the frontier. A modernized cemetery, underdrained, laid off and platted in a skillful and elaborate way, designates a cultured and refined people.

An ornamental burying ground is an imperative demand of progress, and the general desire of the people to keep pace with public sentiment and the onward march of improvement, is consonant to this demand. The urgent necessity for a new cemetery has long been felt by our citizens, and the general welfare of our town; the best interests of business and society have suffered on account of the protracted delay of the enterprise. The repulsive condition of the old cemetery evolved, in part, the plan of the new one, which is emphatically revolutionary in all respects, to the former miscellaneous modes of interment and grotesque ways of caring for lots and graves. The inelegant and promiscuous arrangement of everything, and permanent fixture of boundary lines, within the limits of the old burying ground, proclaimed its eternal divorce from system and beauty; and the only avenue of escape from the painful and distressing incidents, peculiar to such a place, was the founding of a new cemetery, which would be a better place of sepulture and a fitter spot for the habitation of the dead. The inception of Fountain Park Cemetery was not, therefore, premature, but a well timed and carefully matured plan for extricating our citizens from an unhappy dilemma. The success of the undertaking is anticipated by every one; and its completion, in accordance with the designs and desires of the donor, is assured by the kindly drift of public sentiment. The old cemetery, probably, will be speedily vacated, and is destined to become an isolacism, so unlovely that all will shun it, and from the heart of every citizen interested in the welfare of our town will ascend a heartfelt "Amen!"

The Board of Control of Fountain Park Cemetery has adopted such rules and regulations as will prevent any infringement upon the sacredness of the Cemetery by visitors, and guarantee proper decorum in the Park. The donor of these grounds made a very careful and exhaustive examination of all available authorities on the subject of rural cemeteries, and visited many of the best ones in the State in order to familiarize himself with the best and most approved methods of planning and platting a place of burial. Not until he was personally acquainted with the views and opinions of men, recognized as standard authority in such matters, did he commence the establishment of the Park and Cemetery. The rules, limiting the privileges of visitors, were selected with a view to the enhancement of the prosperity of the enterprise, and to throw around it a mantle of protection which would not otherwise exist.

The object of these pages is to give the reader a succint account of the formation of the plans and founding of the Fountain Park Cemetery, a place destined to be the pride and admiration of the present generation, and an honor to posterity.

HISTORICAL.

A brief retrospect reveals the history of the founding of the different cemeteries of Winchester, and the development of the project which led to the purchase of the ground now comprising Fountain Park Cemetery. A recital of the same may be agreeable and instructive.

In the year of 1834, the first regular place of burial was established by one Chas. Conway, then a prominent citizen. The spot designed was situated immediately east of and adjoining the ground now occupied by the Christian church, in Cheney and Watson's addition to the town of Winchester. It was the original intention to locate the cemetery east of Salt Creek, but from some cause the idea was abandoned. The remains buried in this cemetery were subsequently disintered and removed to other places of burial. Ten years later, in the year of 1844, there was a demand, on the part of our citizens, for a new cemetery, and David Heaston allowed them to use a small portion of his land laying southwest from town within a bend of Mud Creek. This selection as a place of burial was a most unfortunate one, and has been attended with unhappy results. For thirty-five or six years this deplorable receptacle was used under protest. The soil was wet and drainage almost impossible, consequently never attempted. During the last few years of its existence public sentiment was aroused to a high degree against it, and a general feeling of dissatisfaction prevailed. Indeed, so intense became the antagonism that many citizens refused to make further use of it, preferring to inhumate their dead at Maxville and other distant cemeteries within the county. The necessity of a better place of sepulture became apparent to all, but to obtain the desired object was a matter of great difficulty. There was an organized effort on the part of citizens, in the fall and winter of 1877, and an earnest endeavor made to induce the Board of Town Trustees to purchase a suitable place for a cemetery, and issue bonds for the payment of the same. A petition was circulated, praying that the Board would take action in the matter and issue the necessary bonds. It was signed by five-eighths of the tax-payers of the town, and presented to the town authorities. After due consideration by that body, a committee, consisting of nine persons, three from each ward, was appointed to select ground for the cemetery. This committee was composed of the following persons, to represent their respective wards: A. Stone, A. Teal and J. J. Cheney, First Ward; J. M. Hodson, R. Bosworth and L. W. Study, Second Ward; T. W. Kizer, J. M. Carver and J. W. Diggs, Third Ward.

The committee never made a report, as a committee, and the Trustees, not caring to assume the responsibility, did not make the purchase. The failure of the project, occurring as it did when public sentiment was clamorous for a solution of the problem, completely disheartened the people, and their friends were dormant upon the subject for some time. The spirit of discontent was not eradicated until after the purchase of the Fountain Park Cemetery grounds by Asahel Stone, who, seeing the extremity of the people, determined to relieve them; and offer, at the same time, a royal tribute to the memory of the dead.

The beautiful tract of ground comprising Fountain Park was purchased from the administrator of Christian Heaston, deceased, at a cost of $4,000, to which was immediately added $300 for a survey and plat. On March 1st, 1880, Gen. A. Stone personally appeared before the Board of Trustees, at a regular monthly meeting, and presented to the town of Winchester, by a deed made to the Board of Trustees, the entire tract of land, for the uses and purposes mentioned in the deed. The Board accepted the donation for the people in the spirit in which it was offered, and immediately appointed Gen. A. Stone, Col. H. H. Neff and T. W. Kizer as a Board of Control for said Cemetery. These gentlemen commenced, at once, a vigorous preparation of the ground for the purposes intended. An itemized statement of the receipts and expenditures of the Board of Control will be found elsewhere in this volume.

The soil of Fountain Park is gravelly, and the face gently undulating, making it highly suitable for a Park and Cemetery. The name is beautifully appropriate and sacredly inspiring. The advantages of Fountain Park in soil, accessibility, appearance, and in affording family unity of interment, without fear of encroachment, are so marked, that its patronage must soon become general. But, when in connection with these influences, we note that the old burying ground has no accommodations for the poor, in the matter of free burial, and the fact that necessity for more ground alone will soon compel the abandonment of the former, and that there is ample provision in the new Cemetery for the free burial of the poor, and sufficient ground to remove any fear or thought of a change for one hundred and fifty years to come, there is nothing left, consistent with reason, to operate in favor of still continuing the old ground.

The location of a Park is a new feature in the geography of our town, nevertheless its advantages and opportunities are manifold and easily understood. It places the citizens of Winchester in rank with those of her sister towns, in public spirit and in those honorable qualities of mind and heart from which springs the desire to provide for the improvement and enjoyment of man's better nature. It advances the social reputation of the town and indicates a spirit of enterprise and progress which is always essential to commercial prosperity. It is a place where all citizens may while away their leisure hours in an enjoyable manner, and to the poor people of our town it is an inestimable blessing, affording as it does a pleasurable place of resort, which, to them, would not otherwise be attainable.

DESCRIPTION.

The following is a correct photograph of the map of said Cemetery, as laid off by Benjamin Grove, Esq., and described by metes and bounds below, and placed on Record in Plat Book No. 1, pages 205 and 206:

I, Asahel Stone, desiring to furnish to the people of Winchester and vicinity a suitable burial place or cemetery, do hereby donate the following real estate for that purpose, viz: The same being in Randolph County, State of Indiana, commencing forty feet west of the quarter-section corner in the line between sections twenty and twenty-nine, township twenty, north of range fourteen east; thence with said section line eighty-six and one-half ($86\frac{1}{2}$) degrees east two hundred and five (205) feet to the turnpike bridge; thence north sixty-four and one-half ($64\frac{1}{2}$) degrees east along the south line of the pike eight hundred (800) feet to a stone; thence south twenty-two and one-half ($22\frac{1}{2}$) degrees east four hundred and seven (407) feet to a stone; thence north twelve and one-half ($12\frac{1}{2}$) degrees east six hundred and three (603) feet to a stone; thence south five (5) degrees east, and continuing along the pike three hundred and sixty-one (361) feet to a stone; thence south eighty-four and one-half ($84\frac{1}{2}$) degrees west ten hundred and twenty-three (1023) feet to the east line of the Cincinnati, Richmond and Ft. Wayne railroad; thence along said railroad and fifty feet east from the center, in a north-westerly direction twelve hundred and thirty-six (1236) feet to a stone; thence north fifteen and one-half (15½) degrees east six hundred and forty-four (644) feet to the place of beginning. All of which is donated to the said town of Winchester, except one lot, which is designated as lot No. 1, in section 19 in the plat of said Cemetery, reserved for myself. The lots, sections, reserves, avenues, alleys, etc., etc., are of the size, description and form as are given in the photograph here filed, and is hereby declared and adopted as the plan and plat of said Cemetery donation.

March 1st, 1880. ASAHEL STONE.

STATE OF INDIANA, RANDOLPH CO., ss.:

Before me, Daniel C. Braden, Recorder in and for said county, personally came Asahel Stone, and acknowledged the exection of the annexed photograph plat for the Fountain Park Cemetery to be his voluntary act and deed, for the purpose and use therein expressed. Witness my hand and seal, this 4th day of March, 1880.

D. C. BRADEN, R. R. C.

(The same being platted, laid off into sections, avenues, reserves, etc., in accordance with the plat herewith filed and recorded. For number of section and number of lots, see plat.)

TERMS OF DONATION.

The said Fountain Park Cemetery shall be governed and controlled by a Board of Control, consisting of three persons, as follows: One of them to be elected by the Trustees of the incorporated town of Winchester, Indiana, or city council of Winchester, when said town shall be incorporated a city, at their first regular meeting in June every third year after the expiration of the term of the first incumbent who is elected and designated as the member elected by the town council until 1883; and the other two to be selected by the lot owners, commencing in the years 1881 and 1882, to serve three years each, and their places to be filled at the expiration of every three years thereafter, so that the term of one member of the Board shall expire each year; each lot owner being entitled to one vote for each twenty-five dollars, or less, that has been paid, and one vote for each additional twenty-five, or less, that has been actually paid. The manner and time of such election to be entirely under the management of the Board of Control, and governed by such rules and regulations as they may make from time to time. All of said Board of Control shall hold their positions until their successors are elected or appointed, and shall have power to fill vacancies. The first Board of Control shall be appointed by the trustees of the town of Winchester: one for the town, to serve three years; one for the lot owners, to serve two years; and one for the lot owners, to serve one year, from the first Monday in June, 1880. It is expected and desired by the undersigned that said Board of Control shall have such powers conferred upon them as will empower them to make all necessary contracts and agreements, with full power to enforce them in law and equity. The duties of said Board of Control, in part, shall be to have entire control of the said Fountain Park Cemetery; to adopt such plans, rules and regulations for the sale of lots and burial places as will probably make them bring the most money, and to see that the full amounts realized for the sale of the lots and burial places, and all other sums from whatever sources received for the Cemetery, shall be judiciously expended in improving and beautifying the said Fountain Park Cemetery. They shall appoint and have control and define the duties of the sexton, or manager, and his assistants, of the Fountain Park Cemetery; and as soon as the funds derived from the sale of lots, or otherwise, shall warrant, they shall erect a cottage house on the lot designated for that purpose, expressly for said sexton. Such police powers shall be conferred upon the sexton and his assistants as will enable him or them to preserve order in and on all parts of said Fountain Park Cemetery, as will protect tombstones, monuments, and any and all other property within the enclosure, or in anywise belonging to the Cemetery, from desecration or injury in any manner; such rules and regulations as may be adopted by the Board of Control for the government and regulation of the sexton and his assistants, with powers, duties, etc.; with regulations for burying persons, and the erection of monuments, tombstones, planting trees, shrubbery, etc., and all other improvements to lots and burial places, and prices that may be charged for digging graves, and such other duties as they may impose upon him and his assistants; also, rules governing the admission of visitors, and all such other rules and duties as may be considered for the best interest of said Fountain Park Cemetery and the lot owners thereof, together with penalties for violating the same, and have said rules printed or painted and at all times kept in a public place in or on said grounds. It is believed that in consideration of the fact that the digging of all graves being given the said sexton, at the prices allowed him by the Board of Control, with a comfortable cottage to live in, with sundry other privileges and profits assigned him, will be a suitable compensation for him for keeping said Fountain Park Cemetery always in good condition, and to the entire satisfaction of the Board of Control and the lot owners. It is, however, intended by the donor of these grounds that this plan is only made as a suggestion, and if any other plan is thought to be better or more efficient in paying for the services of the sexton and assistants, the Board may adopt such plans as they may think best for that purpose.

As soon after the selection of the said Board of Control as practicable, they shall organize by the appointment of one of their number as president, and one of their number as secretary and treasurer, or may appoint the third member a treasurer; and such treasurer may give bonds in such sum as may be required by the Board of Control, with such sureties as they may approve of, conditioned for the faithful performance of his duties as such treasurer, and the honest application of all funds, under the direction of the Board of Control, coming into his hands belonging to the said Fountain Park Cemetery fund. It is expected that all the duties performed and conferred upon the said Board of Control, will be performed cheerfully and without any expense to the said Cemetery fund. The Board of Control shall at all times furnish burial places in which to bury persons who are too poor to pay for the same, free of charge. They shall have an official seal, and shall be fully empowered to make warranty deeds to purchasers of lots and burial places, when the same is fully paid for. All deeds and official papers shall be signed by the president of the Board of Control, and the official seal attached, and the same attested by the secretary.

ASAHEL STONE, Donor.

DEED OF CONVEYANCE.

The following deed of conveyance of Fountain Park Cemetery, to the town of Winchester, Indiana, signed by Asahel Stone and wife, was presented to the Board of Corporation Trustees of the town of Winchester, and accepted by them in trust for the people, March 1st, 1880.

This Indenture Witnesseth, That Asahel Stone and Lydia B. Stone, his wife, of Randolph County, in the State of Indiana, convey and warrant to Asahel Stone, Henry H. Neff and Thomas W. Kizer, Board of Control, in trust, for the town of Winchester, in said county of Randolph and State of Indiana, and their successors forever, whose successors are to be appointed in a manner hereinafter named, the following real estate in Randolph County, Indiana, viz: Commencing forty (40) feet west of the quarter section corner in the line dividing section twenty (20) and twenty-nine (29), in township twenty (20), north of range fourteen (14) east; thence with said section line north eighty-six and one-half degrees ($86\frac{1}{2}°$), two hundred and five feet to the turnpike bridge; thence south sixty-four and one-half degrees ($64\frac{1}{2}°$) east along the south line of the pike, eight hundred (800) feet to a stone; thence south twenty-two and one-half degrees ($22\frac{1}{2}°$) east four hundred and seven (407) feet to a stone;

DEED OF CONVEYANCE.

thence south twelve and one-half degrees ($12\frac{1}{2}°$), east six hundred and three (603) feet to a stone; thence south five degrees (5°) east, and continuing along the pike three hundred and sixty-one feet (361) to a stone; thence south eighty-four and one-half degrees ($84\frac{1}{2}°$) west, ten hundred and twenty-three (1023) feet to the east line of the Cincinnati, Richmond & Fort Wayne Railroad; thence along said railroad and fifty (50) feet east from the center thereof, in a northwesterly direction, twelve hundred and thirty-six (1236) feet to a stone; thence north fifteen and one-half degrees ($15\frac{1}{2}°$) east, six hundred and forty-four (644) feet to the place of beginning.

The said above described real estate is designed and laid off into sections, lots, avenues, drives, alleys, and a park, and fountain, with reserves, etc., etc., by Benjamin Grove, Esq., Civil and Cemetery Engineer, of Louisville, Kentucky, and the same is recorded in Plat Book, page —, and by the grantors donated, free of charge, to the town of Winchester, for the purposes of a cemetery and park, to be known and designated as the Fountain Park Cemetery, and for no other purpose forever; under the following conditions and regulations to be observed, and on failure to comply with the same the property to revert to the said Asahel Stone or his heirs:

The said grounds, now being laid off and platted, and made of record, the same or any part thereof, is never to be altered, changed, or vacated, nor any portion of said premises to be deeded for any other than burial purposes, under the rules heretofore and hereafter set out. Should it be desirous on the part of the Board of Control to change or vacate any of the lots or avenues for the purpose of getting gravel, or making additional reserves, the same may be done by the written consent of the donors or by a majority of the lot owners, with the concurrence of the Town or City Council.

The Fountain Park Cemetery shall be governed in all things by a Board of Control, to be appointed as follows: The first Board of Control to be the persons above named, who are recommended now by the present Trustees for the incorporated town of Winchester. The first one named, Asahel Stone, to serve until the first Monday in June, 1883, and to be designated as the member representing the Town or City Council; at the expiration of the time aforesaid, his successor to be elected by the Town or City Council at their first regular meeting in June, 1883, to serve the Town or City Council for three years. The second one named, Henry H. Neff, to hold his place until June, 1882, and to be designated as one of the members representing the lot owners of said Cemetery, and at the expiration of the time aforesaid, his successor to be elected by the lot owners in such manner and at such time as shall be determined by the Board of Control, to serve for three years; and the third one named, Thomas W. Kizer, to hold his place until June, 1881, and at the expiration of that time, viz: June, 1881, his successor to be elected in all respects as is the second member above named.

All the members of the Board of Control to hold their positions until their successors are elected, and the Board shall fill all vacancies in the Board of Control. Should it be found at any time by the Board of Control that any additional ordinances or laws are required other than herein named, on their request the Town or City Council shall pass such ordinances or laws as are requested by the Board of Control, if in their opinion the same would be for the best interests of said Cemetery. The Board of Control will, as soon as possible, after the acceptance of this deed by the Town Trustees, organize by the appointment of one of their number as president, and one of their number as secretary and treasurer, or may appoint the third member as such treasurer, and may require such treasurer to give bond for the faithful application of all funds coming into his hands as such treasurer. Said Board of Control shall have an official seal, and shall be empowered to make contracts and enforce the same; to make deeds to lots and have the same signed by the president and attested by the secretary, with the official seal attached. Said deeds shall all contain a covenant that the lot owners shall never use or occupy their lots for any other purpose than burial purposes for themselves, their families and relatives, subject to the rules and ordinances adopted by the Board of Control or Town or City Council, and that said lots shall not be sold, transferred or assigned without the consent of the Board of Control, and the erection of monuments, headstones, corner and boundary stones of lots, planting trees and shrubbery, flowers, and doing other improvements on their lots, and all other and further regulations shall be governed by the Board of Control. They shall appoint the sexton or manager, and his deputies, who shall be entirely under their control and subject to their orders, and may be removed by them at any time for cause. The sexton and such of his assistants as the Board of Control may desire, shall be appointed by the Town or City Council, with full police powers to arrest on sight violators of any of the laws or ordinances of said town or city.

The further duties of the Board of Control shall be to have entire control of said Fountain Park Cemetery; to adopt such plans, rules and regulations for the sale of lots and burial places as will probably make them bring the most money, and to see that the full amounts realized for the sale of the lots, and donations, taxes, proceeds from fines, violations of rules and regulations, and from all other sources, which shall be known as the *Fountain Park Cemetery Fund*, shall all be judiciously and honestly expended in improving and beautifying the said Fountain Park Cemetery, and as soon as the funds from the sale of lots, donations or otherwise shall be sufficient to erect on the lot designated in the plat a cottage house for the sexton or superintendent.

The Board of Control shall hereafter be elected from our citizens, who are lot owners, and who will serve cheerfully without pay from, or expense to, the Fountain Park Cemetery Fund.

The Board shall at all times furnish burial places in which to bury persons who are too poor to pay for the same, *free of charge.*

All deeds and official papers shall be signed by the President and attested by the Secretary, with the official seal attached. The Board of Control shall report to the Town or City Council on the first Monday in January, in each year, the financial condition of said Cemetery; the number of lots and burial places sold, with the price received for the same; the amounts expended and for what purposes, and the amount, if any, on hand; and shall report to said Council any other or further items in connection with the Cemetery that said Council may request. The Board of Control shall make rules and regulations in reference to the admission of lot owners, their families and friends, and all other visitors, with the time and manner of the admission of vehicles; time for opening and closing the gates, etc., etc., and such other rules and regulations requiring burial permits; the manner of admitting bodies to the public vault, with cost of the same.

They shall establish a grade of prices for all lots and burial places, and for opening and closing graves, disinterring and re-interring bodies, etc., as shall seem to be necessary for the well-being of a first class cemetery in each and every particular.

It is required of the Board of Trustees of the incorporated town of Winchester, Indiana, to pass ordinances or laws, declaring the following penalties for the violation of any of the hereinafter named misdemeanors or rules and regulations, a fine of five dollars in each case, viz: For riding a horse or horses, or driving a horse or horses faster than a walk in the Cemetery grounds proper; in the Park grounds faster than a trot; for driving on the lots, grass or corner stones of lots; for bringing or using refreshments on any portion of the grounds; for bringing dogs in the grounds; for leaving horses unhitched; for hitching a horse or horses to anything inside the grounds but posts provided for that purpose; for refusing to leave the grounds when ordered to by any officer of the Cemetery, the sexton or his deputies; for violating any of the rules and regulations of the Cemetery; for writing or injuring, or otherwise defacing any monument, tombstone, or other property inside of said Fountain Park Cemetery; for being found in said grounds intoxicated or disturbing the good order and quiet of the place, by noise or other improper conduct; for using profane or indecent language anywhere on the grounds; for plucking or picking flowers, either wild or cultivated, or breaking or injuring any shrub, tree or plant; for firing a gun, revolver or pistol over, across or into, or in any portion of said grounds; for being found anywhere on said grounds with a gun in his possession, (the violations of having and firing guns will not apply to military companies burying with military honors); improper characters, male or female, being found anywhere on said premises, or any person or persons found loitering on said grounds after sunset.

Lot owners, in erecting tombstones, monuments, or in making other improvements on their lots, that shall fail, neglect or refuse to remove the debris, or material or surplus dirt, to any point designated by the sexton, and leave the general surface of the ground as they found it, within a reasonable time after the commencement of the work, shall be notified by the sexton, and if not complied with in a reasonable time, said lot owner shall be fined five dollars for each day said obstruction is allowed to remain; and the sexton may remove the same at any time at the expense of the owner of the lot, who will also be responsible to adjoining lot owners for any injury that may be done to their lot or lots by the party or parties aforesaid.

Lot owners refusing to plant cut stones or marble, not less than six inches square and octagonal on top, not less than twenty-one inches long, and set in the ground firmly, so as not to be more than three inches above the surface of the ground, designating the corners and boundaries of their lots, when notified by the sexton and not complying with said notice within a reasonable time, shall be fined five dollars, and the Board of Control may have the same planted at the expense of said lot owner. All of the fines collected as above shall be for the benefit of the Fountain Park Cemetery fund.

The grounds hereinbefore described, which are hereby dedicated and donated and named the FOUNTAIN PARK CEMETERY, shall be embraced and included within the corporate limits of the town of

DEED OF CONVEYANCE.

Winchester, Randolph county, Indiana. The grantors herein named make one reservation in this general deed, to-wit: Lot No. one (1), in section No. nineteen (19), as is laid off, platted and numbered on said plat, as of record aforesaid, for a burial place for themselves, family and relatives.

In witness whereof, the said Asahel Stone and Lydia B. Stone, his wife, have hereunto set their hands and seals this 1st day of March, 1880.

ASAHEL STONE, [SEAL.]
LYDIA B. STONE, [SEAL.]

STATE OF INDIANA, RANDOLPH COUNTY, SS.:

Before me, James S. Engle, a Notary Public in and for said county, this, the 1st day of March, 1880, Asahel Stone and Lydia B. Stone, his wife, acknowledged the execution of the annexed deed.

Witness my hand and notarial seal, this 1st day of March, 1880.

JAMES S. ENGLE, Notary Public.

THE PRESENTATION.

To the Honorable Board of Trustees of the Incorporated Town of Winchester, Indiana:

Mr. C. E. Magee, President of the Board of Trustees of the Incorporated Town of Winchester, Randolph County, Indiana, and John W. Diggs, Esq., and Samuel D. Fox, Esq., Trustees of said Town.

Gentlemen:— For a number of years I have, in common with the most of our citizens, felt the importance of having a suitable and respectable cemetery located near our town, of sufficient size to accommodate the wants of this community for a great many years to come, laid out with taste and modern engineering skill and improvement, into sections, lots, and other burial places, driveways, alleys, etc.; with all necessary arrangements to have the same always kept in good condition; to be in all respects a suitable place of burial for ourselves and others. "And as others have done, we should set apart a spot of earth to hold the dust that once was Love," and engage art and wealth in its adornment. And we would beautify the quiet homes of our dead, whose bright pictures hang in the silent halls of memory and whose names we will cherish forever. Next to our hearth-stones, around which cluster the dearest joys of life, should come the final resting place of our dead. It is barbarous to give the loved and unforgotten to the rank weeds and to the hand of desecration, as if they held no place in our affections. Let us make a home for them, as beautiful as a dream, which shall last as long as the stars shine, or the river rolls its bright waters to the sea. The place should be made so attractive that affection will make repeated and delighted visits there, and around which memory, even from distant lands, will fondly linger. We will adorn with flowers and shrubs these winding ways and grassy walks, and hang upon these urns garlands of love and friendship. The pearly dawn will spread its light over these green hillocks, and the last beams of departing day will kiss these white monuments and leave a blessing behind it. Then night and silence will follow, and the moon and stars with their mellow radiance will embalm the city of the dead. It is a pleasure to have a personal interest in such beautiful grounds, and it is a solemn duty that we owe the dead to provide for them a final home.

Every one in all this country should purchase one of these lots — as every dollar received for the sale of lots is expended in improving and beautifying the grounds — and set it apart for himself and family. If necessary, we should part with the luxuries of life, nay, trench upon its very necessities, mortgage our surplus lands, to make the investment. By all means, at any reasonable sacrifice, let us secure a bit of earth in which to bury our dead. For the purpose of furnishing such a place, I have purchased forty acres of ground south of and adjoining town, lying between the Cincinnati, Richmond and Fort Wayne railroad and the Lynn and Winchester turnpike, a location that would never be required for the extension of the town limits. The eastern portion of the land lies from fifteen to twenty-five feet above the bottom of the creek. On the western side the land is gently undulating, shedding towards the west, or railroad. These grounds are believed to be the best that could be selected for the purpose anywhere in this vicinity, and very suitably situated for a cemetery. On the western side of these grounds is a strip of land the entire length of the tract, which is too low for burial purposes, which I think very well adapted for a park; and when completed, with its avenues, walks, flowers, shrubs, trees and fountain, will be a most lovely place of resort for our people, in all suitable weather. The map of the ground, which I now exhibit and present, was drawn with scientific care by a competent cemetery engineer of Louisville, Kentucky, Benjamin Grove, Esq., which shows that when completed as per plan, the FOUNTAIN PARK CEMETERY will be one of the finest burial places in Eastern Indiana. These grounds I desire to donate to you, in trust for the people, believing this to be the best plan to carry out my original design, long in contemplation, for furnishing a suitable burying place for our departed friends. My ideas and plans are more fully set out in the other papers which I herewith submit.

I trust, gentlemen, that you will accept this donation for the people, and in their interests carry out the plans and ideas of the donor, and pass such ordinances or laws as will fully enforce all the rules and regulations adopted by the Board of Control, and make such proper police regulations as will insure their prompt enforcement. Should you accept this offer in the spirit in which it is made, and enter upon the duties therein expressed in the papers referred to, I shall most cheerfully deed the same to you and your successors, believing that I have simply performed a duty which I owe to myself and family and friends and posterity. I shall except from this general deed one lot, (No. 1, in section 19,) for myself and family and relatives, as our last resting place.

ASAHEL STONE, Donor.

Winchester, Ind., March 1, 1880.

PETITION TO ANNEX TERRITORY
TO THE TOWN OF WINCHESTER.

Come now Charles E. Magee, Samuel D. Fox and John W. Diggs, Trustees of the incorporated town of Winchester, and present their petition herein to the Board, praying for the annexation to said incorporation of contiguous territory, which petition is in these words, to-wit:

STATE OF INDIANA, RANDOLPH CO., ss.:

To the Honorable Board of Commissioners of the County of Randolph: The undersigned, constituting the Board of Trustees of the town of Winchester, in Randolph county, Indiana, would, for and in behalf of said town, most respectfully petition your honorable body to annex the following described real estate in Randolph county, Indiana, to-wit: Commencing forty-six (46) feet west in the quarter section corner, in the line dividing sections twenty (20) and twenty-nine (29), in Township 20 north, of Range 14 east; thence with said section line north eighty-six and one-half degrees ($86\frac{1}{2}°$) east two hundred and five feet, to the Winchester and Lynn pike bridge; thence south $64\frac{1}{2}$ degrees east along the south line of the pike, 800 feet, to a stone; thence south $22\frac{1}{2}$ degrees east 407 feet, to a stone; thence south $12\frac{1}{2}$ degrees east 603 feet, to a stone;

PETITION TO ANNEX TERRITORY.

thence south 5 degrees east, and continuing along the pike, 361 feet, to a stone; thence south 84½ degrees west 1,023 feet, to the east line of the Cincinnati, Richmond and Fort Wayne Railroad; thence along said railroad, and fifty feet east from the center thereof, in a northwesterly direction, 1,236 feet, to a stone; thence north 15½ degrees east 644 feet, to the place of beginning. Your petitioners would further show that said real estate is contiguous to and adjoining the corporate limits of the town of Winchester, and is not platted or laid off into lots in any way whatever; and the reason of asking the annexation of said territory is that the same is to be donated to the town of Winchester by Asahel Stone for the purpose of being used for a cemetery for said town; and that we ask that the same be annexed so as to give said town power to exercise and have public powers over said cemetery grounds. A plat accurately describing said territory proposed to be attached by metes and bounds, is filed with this petition, and marked Exhibit A, and made a part of this petition.

CHAS. E. MAGEE,
JOHN W. DIGGS,
SAMUEL D. FOX.

Trustees of the Town of Winchester.

STATE OF INDIANA, RANDOLPH COUNTY, ss.:

Being duly sworn, say upon oath that the matters and things set forth in the above petition are true and correct. L. W. STUDY.

Subscribed and sworn to before me, this the 24th day of February, 1880. J. W. MACY, Clerk.

Said petitioners also filed answer of A. Stone, which is in these words, to-wit:

STATE OF INDIANA, RANDOLPH COUNTY, ss.:
In the Commissioners' Court, March Term, 1880.

In the matter of the petition of the town of Winchester to annex contiguous territory, comes now Asahel Stone, who is the owner of all the real estate described and set out in the petition and asked to be annexed to the town of Winchester, and for his answer says that he gives his consent to said annexation of said territory, and makes no objection thereto, and waives all right of notice by publication or otherwise. ASAHEL STONE.

And the Board of County Commissioners, having seen and examined said petition, and having heard the evidence of witnesses, and having carefully examined the plat of the territory petitioned to be annexed to the town of Winchester; also, having examined answer of A. Stone, waiving right of notice by publication or otherwise, and being satisfied with the matters and things contained and set forth in said petition and answer, and that the law has been complied with as required in such cases, order and direct that the territory as heretofore described, be and is hereby annexed to said town of Winchester, and made a part of the corporate limits thereof. E. F. HOLLIDAY,
WILSON ANDERSON,
WILLIAM BOTKIN,
Commissioners of Randolph County.

RESOLUTIONS OF ACCEPTANCE.

The following resolutions were passed by the Board of Trustees of the town of Winchester, March 1st, 1880:

Resolved, By the Board of Trustees of the town of Winchester: That said town does hereby accept the deed made by Asahel Stone and wife to said town, for the purpose of making a cemetery, on the terms and conditions therein set forth.

Resolved, By the Board of Trustees of the town of Winchester: That the following territory adjoining the corporate limits of the town of Winchester be and is hereby taken into and included within the corporate limits of the town of Winchester, and made subject to all the ordinances and by-laws of said town, now in force, to-wit: Commencing forty feet west of the quarter section corner, in section line between sections twenty (20) and twenty-nine (29), township twenty (20), north of range fourteen (14) east; thence with said section line north eighty-six and one-half degrees ($86\frac{1}{2}°$) east 205 feet to the turnpike bridge; thence south sixty-four and one-half degrees ($64\frac{1}{2}°$) east along the south line of the said Lynn and Winchester turnpike eight hundred feet to a stone; thence south twenty-two and one-half degrees ($22\frac{1}{2}°$) east 407 feet to a stone; thence south twelve and one-half degrees (12½°) east 603 feet to a stone; thence south five degrees (5°) east 361 feet to a stone; thence south eighty-four and one-half degrees (84½°) west one thousand and twenty-three feet (1023) to the east line of the Cincinnati, Richmond & Fort Wayne Railroad; thence along said railroad and fifty feet from the center thereof, in a northwesterly direction twelve hundred and thirty-six feet (1236) to a stone; thence north fifteen and one-half degrees (15°) east 644 feet to the place of beginning.

DEDICATION OF FOUNTAIN PARK CEMETERY.

On Saturday, July 3d, 1880, the establishment of Fountain Park Cemetery was consummated by a most impressive ceremonial dedication. It was a glorious day, and to those who participated in the pleasures and sublimity of the occasion, its memory will be sacred. At an early hour in the morning the streets of Winchester were lined with citizens and country people, many of the latter named having left the plow and reaper to share the mutual fruition of the day and attest their cordial approbation.

A procession formed about 10:30 o'clock, and proceeded to the cemetery grounds, headed by a band of music. The orders of Odd Fellows, Masons and Knights of Honor were represented. The Odd Fellows numbered about 75; the Masons 60, including 16 Knights Templar; the Knights of Honor 25. Following these came a great concourse of people—on foot, on horseback, in buggies, carriages, farm wagons, spring wagons, and other vehicles—the whole forming a vast, royal holiday pageant, worthy of the occasion. Arriving at the Cemetery, the members of the Masonic fraternity formed a circle at the command of the Grand Marshal, Col. Cranor. After prayer by Rev. R. D. Spellman, A. Q. Marsh, representative of the Grand Master of the Grand

Lodge of Masons of Indiana, solemnly dedicated the Cemetery to the repose of the dead and the care of the living. The Masons then retired, and Rev. B. F. Foster, Grand Secretary of the Grand Lodge of I. O. O. F. of this State, dedicated the Cemetery with the beautiful ceremony of that order; after which, the procession reformed and marched to Carter's Grove.

The afternoon session was opened with prayer by Rev. P. Carland. Col. H. H. Neff, Secretary of the Board of Control, then read the following report:

For many years the citizens of Winchester felt the want of suitable grounds convenient to town for the interment of their departed friends. No feasible plan seemed to be devised by our town authorities for the consummation of any method to meet this pressing want. Fortunately for our town and its citizens, we have in our midst a liberal hearted and enterprising citizen, with ample means, who, in the nobleness of his generous nature, realized the necessity for immediate action in this important matter, and matured a plan by which the desired object would be obtained. And in order to carry out his noble purpose, he purchased from the administrator of the estate of Christian Heaston, deceased, a tract of land containing forty acres, suitably located for the purpose, and convenient to town, at a cost of $4,000; and, also at his own expense, procured a survey and plat of the grounds, at a cost of $300, having procured for this purpose the services of Benjamin Grove, Esq., of Louisville, Kentucky, an engineer who stands unrivaled in topographical

DEDICATION.

and landscape surveying, having had long and extensive experience in laying out ornamental cemeteries.

On the 1st day of March, 1880, Gen. Stone conveyed by warranty deed the entire tract of forty acres to the trustees of the town of Winchester, and their successors, to be held and used by them perpetually as a cemetery, and requested the Trustees to appoint a Board of Control to take charge of and control the same, for the uses and purposes expressed in the deed of conveyance, and on the first day of March, 1880, the Trustees appointed Asahel Stone, H. H. Neff and T. W. Kizer a Board of Control, who immediately organized by the election of a President, Secretary and Treasurer, as provided for in the deed of conveyance.

The Board was without any available means to commence the work of preparing the grounds for use as contemplated by the donor, but were relieved from this dilemma by the generous proposition of Gen. Stone, the donor, to loan the Board one thousand dollors, without interest, until such time as that amount could be realized from the sale of lots. With this liberal and timely aid the Board resolved to commence work without delay, and immediately put a considerable force of laborers at work ditching, tiling, excavating and filling. A considerable delay, however, was caused by the continual wet weather, and the difficulty, at times, of securing a sufficient force of laborers. The one thousand dollars furnished by Gen. Stone was soon exhausted, and the Board was under the necessity

DEDICATION.

of suspending the work or resort to borrowing more money. The latter expedient was resorted to, and the Board negotiated for $1,000 more on liberal terms. With this amount the work has been prosecuted up to the present time, trusting that the liberality and public spirit of our citizens will not be wanting in sustaining this noble enterprise, and aiding liberally in carrying out the praiseworthy design of Gen. Stone in making Fountain Park Cemetery a place of beauty and a fit receptacle for the remains of departed friends. Every dollar that is realized from .the sale of lots will be expended in beautifying and keeping in good repair, the cemetery grounds. It is hoped that our citizens will purchase lots without delay, and thus enable the Board to prosecute the work of final completion as soon as possible.

The following is the account of the expenditures for labor, etc.:

Ditching, 450 rods	$ 640 54
Tiling, 505 rods	205 20
Excavating, Grading and Filling	844 44
Ornamental and Shade Trees	97 12
Transportation on same	5 76
Hedgeing	43 25
Records and Seal	20 00
Grass Seed	9 25
Labor on Ground, prior to May 8th	134 44
Balance due Engineer, not paid	300 00
	$2,300 00
Money borrowed and paid out	2,000 00
Balance unpaid	$ 300 00

H. H. NEFF, Secretary.

June 3d, 1880.

DEDICATION CEREMONIES
—OF—
FOUNTAIN PARK CEMETERY.
(Selected.)

Read by B. F. Foster, G. S., in behalf of the Independent Order of Odd Fellows.

As Abraham bought the field of Ephrou, with its adornment of trees and the cave of Machpelah, that he might make a burial place for his dead, so have you set apart these grounds, as the spot in which the dust of your kindred, and your own, shall return to the earth as it was.

Not as a desert waste shall it ever be suffered to lie open, nor become like the garden of the slothful, overgrown with weeds and with walls broken down; but the winds of heaven that pass over it in the season of bloom, shall be laden with fragrance; and in the winter time they shall sigh the memory of the departed through the branches of the evergreens.

Not as implying holiness in anything material, nor as imparting sanctity by a ceremonial, are we about to dedicate this place of burial. All that shall be brought hither will be of the earth, earthy; yet even the body, in its silence and dust, may claim peculiar respect as having been the tabernacle of a spirit that shall never die.

It is not superstition, but religion, which subdues us into the stillness of awe in the presence of death, and impels us reverently to regard the insensible form, not because of what it is, but because of what it was. The reverential sentiment is passed over to the earth to which it is returned, and the burial place thus becomes invested with the solemnity of holy ground.

When, therefore, the light and life of infancy, or childhood, shall fade away into the morning radiance of the spiritual sun, hither shall you come, to commit the body to its serene repose, sorrowing that earth has one mortal less, yet rejoicing that heaven has one angel more. The silver cord hath been loosed.

Earth to earth, ashes to ashes, dust to dust.

When youth, or early manhood, or womanhood, shall perish in the promise or joy of usefulness, there will be sore lamentation at the springs of social life; and the wail will here be renewed when the stricken form is laid in the pulseless heart of our common mother. The pitcher hath been broken at the fountain.

Earth to earth, ashes to ashes, dust to dust.

When the dial shall be darkened at meridian, because the maturity of life has passed away into the mystery of death, the funeral dirge will penetrate this shadowy silence with its mournful chords, and the heart-aching of sympathy shall respond to the heart-breaking of woe. The golden bowl hath been broken.

Earth to earth, ashes to ashes, dust to dust.

When the weary pilgrim of many years, stepping out of the solemn procession of life, shall have put off his sandals, and laid aside his staff, and been gathered into the promised rest, hither shall you bring all that was mortal, and reverently consign it to the house appointed for all the living. The wheel hath been broken at the cistern.

Earth to earth, ashes to ashes, dust to dust.

Thus do we dedicate and devote these grounds to the purpose of burial. Let no unseemly mirth invade this sanctuary of the dead, nor let such as come hither to weep, or who shall remember this place of graves, abandon themselves to hopeless sorrow.

In the vision of Christian faith, time is that section of eternity with which we have to do in the flesh, and immortality is but the continuous life, when time shall be no more. There is no death to one who has triumphed over it by the power of a living trust in God, for death is only in the darkness which comes forth of the tomb, and gathers around the hidden path into the life to come. We are pilgrims and strangers in the earth; our citizenship is in the invisible and eternal Presence.

We see not the value of this revelation, or regard it not, when the sky is cloudless, and the joy of the heart is looking out of undimmed eyes; but when the heavens are robed in gloom, and the soul is bowed in bereavement, a beam of light breaks through a rift in the cloud, and the mourner looks up, and is glad, because through tears he beholds the rainbow of hope spanning the abyss of death. The earth, once clad in beauty and lately clothed in sack-cloth, is now hallowed by the ministering spirits of the Most High, and even the darkness of midnight is lighted up by the glories of eternal noon.

The sundered silver cord of childhood, the crystal pitcher marred in youth, the perished golden bowl of middle life, and the broken wheel of old age — all these types shall come to us in the subduing realities of the world; but this dedication is not completed with lifeless symbols, nor ended in earth, and ashes, and dust.

Recollection will indeed cling to the once visible form, and mourning affection will seek the living among the dead; but remembrance, when transfigured by the angel of hope, will demand the associations of cheerfulness.

Wherefore, let buds, and blossoms, and flowers, and evergreens, be strewn on the graves which await our coming; though bloom may perish, and verdure pass away, the memory of fragrance and beauty will consecrate this place, and sweetly blend with the prophecy of an undying life.

"And darkness and doubt are now fleeing away,
    No longer we wane in conjecture forlorn;
So breaks on the traveler — faint and astray —
    The bright and the balmy effulgence of morn.
See truth, love and mercy, in triumph descending,
    And nature all glowing in Eden's first bloom;
On the cold cheek of death smiles and roses are blending,
    And beauty immortal awakes from the tomb."

And now, in the name of "Friendship, Love and Truth," and "Faith, Hope and Charity," I declare these grounds set apart for the purposes for which they were donated, the burial of the dead.

BENEDICTION.

Now the God of Peace, who brought again from the dead our Lord Jesus, that great Shepherd of the sheep, through the blood of the everlasting covenant, make you perfect in every good work to do His will, working in you that which is well pleasing in His sight, through Jesus Christ, to whom be glory forever. Amen.

Address of Hon. Thomas M. Browne,

— AT THE —

Dedication of Fountain Park Cemetery,

JULY 3d, 1880.

Ladies and Gentlemen:

It is said by Fuller, that when presents were made they should be of such things as "would last long," so they would be "in some sort immortal," constantly refreshing the memory. Of this sort is the munificent donation of Fountain Park Cemetery, for it will be a monument of the taste, the appreciation of the beautiful, and the generosity of our distinguished fellow-citizen, until the granite columns that may rise from its bosom shall crumble into sands. The name of the donor will be interlinked with the gift, and be held in grateful remembrance by every sorrowing heart who comes here to drop a tear or breathe a prayer over the grave that holds some loved form in its relentless embrace. It is a most generous gift, and we are assembled here to-day to expresss our gratitude for it, and to formally and appropriately dedicate it. We come here to dedicate this earth, these walks, these trees, these picturesque grounds, for all time, as a burial place of the dead. Soon the hearse, with its mournful cortege, will come here,

DEDICATION CEREMONIES.

and here will be made the quiet grave. Here the hand of affection will plant the flower and the evergreen. Here the tranquil bark will ride at anchor without a disturbing wave. No storms will beat against the life that lies here. Beneath the gentle undulatious that will rise upon this earth, the little child will nestle as quietly as if it slept on its mother's bosom. Here the hand of the artisan will forget its cunning, and the brain of the thinker be racked by no disturbing thought. The hero of the battle-field will lie here with broken sword and shield, conquered at last. And here, in unepitaphed tombs, in the shadows of these trees or in the glare of the sunlight, the weary heart, broken by suffering, will find a balm for its woes. All will come here to rest at last. The pale mother will come with her new born babe; the bright and joyous boy will leave top and bat and merry group of playmates, and come, and with him will come the strong youth just reaching man's estate, the maiden just blossoming into beautiful womanhood, the strong man in the high noon of his manhood, and halting and trembling old age. In this last earthly abode they will all be equal forever. The grave is the mighty leveler. In it the rich and the poor, the prince and the peasant, the king and the subject, are peers. There the malignant heart is pulseless and the slanderous tongue is still. "There all the flames of rage are extinguished, hatred is appeased, and angelic pity, like a weeping sister, bends with gentle and close embrace over the funeral urn." In it there is neither envy nor ambition nor hatred. As a resort of the living and a habitation of the dead, we devote and consecrate these grounds.

"This fairest spot of hill and glade,
  Where blooms the flower and waves the tree,
And silver streams delight the shade,
  We consecrate, O death! to thee.

"Here all the months the year may know,
  Shall watch this 'Eden of the dead,'
To wreathe with flowers or crown with snow,
  The dreamless sleeper's narrow bed.

"And when above its graves we kneel,
  Resigning to the mouldering urn
The friends whose silent hearts shall feel
  No balmy summer's glad return,

"Each marble shaft our hands may rear
  To mark where dust to dust is given,
Shall lift its chiselled column here,
  To point our tearful eyes to Heaven."

Reverence for the dead has marked every age, is characteristic of almost every race and every religion. Savage and civilized, Pagan and Christian, alike adopt some method by which they testify their love or admiration for the life that is gone out. The tomb to which the lifeless body has been consigned, or the urn in which its ashes are garnered, is esteemed a sacred place in which affection has treasured up its loved and lost. There, around tomb and urn, love plants its gentle flower, and there it builds its graceful monument.

The ancient Egyptians embalmed their dead so they could be kept for generations, as a sacred trust, in their very households. The early Greeks and Romans adopted the Phrygian custom of incremating their dead, and depositing their ashes in commemorative urns, which they guarded with pious care. Our custom of burying in the open fields and marking the place of interment with monument of wood, or bronze, or stone, ante-dates by centuries the Christian era. The Hebrews, Babylonians, Greeks, Romans and Egyptians had their public burial grounds. Jerusalem had its cemetery in the classic valley of Cedron, and the Appian Way, in the days of Appius Claudius, three centuries before Christ, was skirted on either side by the burial places of Rome. Four thousand years and more ago the great Pyramids of the valley of the Nile were built as tombs for Cheops and Cephron and other monarchs of Meroe and Ethiopia. Temples and churches, Pagan and Christian, have been consecrated as resting places for the dead. The Pantheon at Rome, the grandest achievement of ancient architecture, is no longer the mere temple of the mythical gods, but stands a monument to its honored dead. Under its great domes and porticos, and within the area circled by its grand columns of granite, are mouldering the remains of the immortal Raphael and Carracci. Pisa has its *Campo Santo* — the beautiful city of the dead, and Paris has its no less attractive and historic *Pere la Chaise*. In France, in Italy, in England, and indeed wherever in civilized lands death has claimed a subject, there are hallowed burial places. Go to London and you will find the venerable St. Paul's and the grand and historic

Westminster Abbey, little else than monuments to departed genius and heroism. There, under the dome of St. Paul's, side by side, lie Nelson and Wellington — the hero of Trafalgar and the hero of Waterloo; and near them one greater than they, Howard, the philanthropist, who invaded dungeons, went into the huts of squalid poverty, and challenged death in infected hospitals, that he might minister to human want and alleviate human suffering. And that most venerated fabric of the English Church, Westminster Abbey, is but the sepulchre of Kings and the resting place of famous Englishmen from every rank and creed and form of genius. Here the dust of kings, warriors, statesmen, poets; that of the royal Tudors, Stuarts, and Plantagenets; of the Henrys, Elizabeth, and Mary, mingle with that of Chatham, Fox, Castlereigh, Hastings, Macaulay, Chaucer and Spenser. But England's grand names are not all inscribed at St. Paul's and Westminster, for Shakespeare, Wordsworth, Southey, Scott, Burns, and a host of others little less conspicuous in the annals of Great Britain, slumber here and there, far away from these gray old piles, in the quiet village and country kirk-yard, amid the scenes they knew and loved. Like the great Burke, these men preferred "a sunny corner in a country church-yard to the tomb of the Capulets." We have no cathedrals or monumental grounds dating back in the centuries, but we point with pride to Greenwood, to Oak Hill, to Mt. Auburn, to Springdale, to Laurel Hill, to Arlington — beautiful as Eden — and to the thousands of modest church yards, clustering around every village and resting on almost every hill side, where, in the midst of rose, and honeysuckle, and cedar, the granite or marble shaft stands solemn sentinel over the lowly habitations of the dead. And we, too, have Mt. Vernon and Marshfield, Monticello and Ashland, consecrated by a nation's tears, for in those hallowed spots sleep Washington and Webster, Jefferson and Clay, illustrious men— men whose genius and patriotism have given American courage and statesmanship a conspicuous page in the annals of the world.

But who, at the end of the race, will come to lay down their weary burdens and seek rest in the beautiful grounds we dedicate to-day? Who can name them, who write the story of their lives or death? The plumed hero, whose ear has been gladdened by the applause of the multitude; the statesman, who has fashioned statutes and charters of human liberty; the orator, whose matchless eloquence has moved listening senates; the martyr, who has sacrificed everything but conscience for his cause, may come and pillow their heads here. And

> "Some village Hamden, with that dauntless breast
>   The little tyrant of his fields withstood;
> Some mute, inglorious Milton here may rest;
>   Some Cromwell, guiltless of his country's blood."

Here may be laid the miser, who clutched his gold while he starved both body and soul, and at his side the good, generous man whose hands were as

"Open as day for melting charity."

Here may be buried men too weak to win in the battle of life, and with them, and alike forgotten,

"Hands the rod of empire might have swayed."

Every sex, age and condition must come to this end at last, for "it is appointed unto all men once to die." Death will not be bribed. It will touch the harp and it will be unstrung; the lip, and it will be mute; the heart, and it will be stilled; the eye, and it will be sightless; the brain, and it will no longer be haunted by dreams of fame and power. We do not know when the summons will come, but it is certain that in an hundred years from now all those who hear me to-day will have passed away. We know the end is certain, inevitable; and beyond this how little we know of death. The curtains of the grave are inpenetrable, and no eye, save that of faith, has seen beyond them. We have measured the distances of the planets, and sounded the depths of the seas; the winds and steam and the lightnings have been made the active and submissive agents of our will; and the very heavens above us and the earth beneath have been by science despoiled of their secrets. We read the history of the countless centuries of the past in the rocks. We mark the coming of the comet and the eclipse to the fraction of a second. The seeming possibilities of the past are the easy accomplishments of to-day. Every hour since God said, "Let there be light, and there was light," has been signalized by the discovery of some hidden truth. Day by day, Nature has been opening up its treasures and increasing the fountains of human knowledge and strengthening the foundations of human faith. Onward with unfaltering step has been the march of human progress, until we have attained a height of intellectual development never approached before. Science, with telescope and laboratory and compass, has been busy with the earth and water, air and light — with the oceans and the stars — until their mysteries stand revealed. And yet much has been withheld. There are mysteries science has not solved — mysteries that defy human philosophy and perplex human faith. What, with all that science has achieved, do we know of the origin of life and the awful mystery of death and human destiny? How these problems defy demonstration and invite speculation. Who will tell what life is, whence it comes, whither it goes? And yet life is everywhere. It is, in its countless forms, in the earth, the air, and the seas. It inhabits the insect as well as the ox. It is said there are animalcule so small that it takes one hundred and fifty millions of them to weigh a grain, and yet they are as instinct with life as "the whale that seems an island as it sleeps on the waves." The living creatures of to-day, yesterday were not. The consciousness of to-day, yesterday was all unconscious. The time was when the black night of utter unconsciousness imprisoned our every thought, feeling, emotion. What architect touched this state of nothingness and made it instinct with life? By what alchemy was sensation, spirit, communicated to gross, lifeless matter? What law directed the operations of the invisible but intelligent force that developed matter into the living, reasoning man? All forms of matter have been put into the alembic — have been separated and recombined; but who has been able to analyze that invisible, spiritual phenomenon, life? Chemists have experimented for years, and have been unable to embody in matter sensation, or life, in its lowest and crudest form. Scientists speak of "protoplasms," "the immaterial principle," of "primordial germs," of "evolution," and the "survival of the fittest," only to prove that science, as to this great question, is still groping in the regions of doubt and conjecture. The *savans*, after all their research, and all their logic, have left us in distressing darkness, and at last we fall back on a faith that is above philosophy: "that this tangled skein is in the hands of One who saw the end from the beginning," and who will, in the fullness of the appointed time, unravel all.

There is a truth no man can challenge; there is an intelligent cause governing all created things. The evidence of this is found in every object about us. It is proven by the wonderful adaptation of every created thing to a purpose, by the harmonious relation of things to each other, and the intelligence and completeness of the universe as a whole. The scientists call this intelligent creative power, Law — the Christian calls it God. It is not my purpose to take up this issue. For myself I can say that it is more difficult for me to comprehend the existence of a force in matter by which certain particles are evolved into brutes and others into men, than it is to understand the presence and guidance of a reasoning, omnipotent mind, who creates and then governs by the exercise of a supreme will. A self-existent God is as possible as self-existent matter.

But we know we live, and we know we must die. This thought is brought forcibly to our minds on an occasion like this. Every tombstone, every little grave under the green sward, is a sermon teaching its impressive lesson. It reminds us that life is short, that in its duration it is but so many heart throbs, that from the cradle to the grave it is measured by mere pulsations. Every breath we breathe brings us closer and closer upon eternity, and every step we take but shortens the way that leads to the end of the journey. How true it is that, second by second, we are drifting down toward that dark sea whose depths have never been fathomed and whose shores have never been explored.

Brief as this life is, we may so shape it that our individual influence will be felt long after our "bodies sleep under the violets." It has been four thousand years since Homer wrote, but the Iliad and Odyssey are in their infancy. They have a perpetual youth. How long will the philosophy of Confucius, of Plato, of Aristotle — the verse of Shakespeare, of Cowper, of Whittier, of Moore, of Burns, and of Longfellow survive them? For how many generations to come will Scott, and Bulwer, and George Eliot be read? When, think you, the world will forget the name of Washington, of Howard, of Wilberforce, of Lincoln? The fame of Raphael and Michel Angelo will be fresh when the last trace of their immortal paintings has disappeared from fresco and canvas forever. The great and generous in thought and action do not perish. The victories won by Watts, and Fulton, and Stephenson, and Franklin, and Morse, over steam and electricity, will be felt by mankind to the "last syllable of recorded time." Man dies, but his deeds live. His good deeds "will be as legible on the hearts he leaves behind as the stars on the brow of evening." It is a cynical view of life to regard it "a tale told by an idiot, full of sound and fury, signifying nothing." It is, on the contrary, a season given us in which to work and achieve, not for to-day and ourselves only, but for all humanity and for all time. In the words of Carlyle: "Thy life, wert thou the pitifullest of all the sons of men, is no idle dream, but a solemn reality. It is thy own; it is all thou hast to front eternity with. Work then, like a star, unhasting yet unresting." Let us work, then, remembering that life is short, that it is but a shadow, that the moment that is past comes not again, that the hand can never be turned back on the dial. Let us work, then, faithfully, for the step once taken can never be retraced, and the mistakes we make can never be fully repaired. Let us work, then, knowing moreover that sin dwarfs and disfigures the moral nature, that it "kills the optic nerve of the soul and puts out the moral eyesight;" that it blots from the moral sky the star of hope, and leaves the human soul in a rayless night. Let us

> "Live in deeds, not years — in thoughts, not breaths —
> In feeling, not in figures on a dial;
> We count the time by heart-throbs. He most lives
> Who thinks most, feels noblest, acts the best."

But what of immortality! "Does death end all?" Does it paralyze the soul? Does it destroy consciousness and utterly put out the faculties! Or is it not rather a mere physical change by which the soul is relieved from its burden of sensual passions, that it may leap upward into spiritual light and life? Is it true, as some would teach us, that we are all afloat on a trackless sea — with no chart or compass to direct, at the mercy of the winds and waves; with no destination, but simply drifting about, hopelessly and aimlessly, until some rude storm wrecks us, and our bark goes down in the fathomless waters without the hope of resurrection? Because these men cannot cast the telescope and sweep that future beyond the grave, as they do the planets or the distant mountain tops, they tell us that death is an oblivion — protracted and endless. They demand some proof, some demonstration. They tell us that none come back to whisper even the faintest word of hope to the soul struggling with this great problem. True,

> "None return from those quiet shores,
>   Who cross with the boatman, cold and pale;
> We hear the dip of the golden oars,
>   And catch the gleam of the snowy sail,"

and then the voyager passes out of sight; but because we see no returning sail, shall we believe it has gone down in endless night? May we not still have faith that it has anchored at the other shore?

Even aside from revelation, we have reason to hope a future life. That spirit is immortal, has been the almost unchallenged conviction of the master minds of all ages, and the bed-rock of every system of religion. Heathen and Christian have built their systems upon this faith. The heathen Cicero, living a hundred years before Christ, died inspired with an unfaltering belief that he would "meet Cato in the divine assembly and company of the spirits." Evidence of immortality is found in the universal desire for it in the human heart. It is an appetite of the soul. Leigh Hunt puts the argument in an interrogatory: "Has nature, who quenches our bodily thirst, who rests our weariness, and who perpetually encourages us to endeavor onwards, prepared no food for this appetite for immortality?" For physical thirst and hunger, God has made ample provision; has he neglected the spiritual? There is no capacity for attachment without some object to love, and it is against all logic to say that the universal craving for eternal life has no immortality to satisfy the want. Human nature is made up by wants on one side and supply on the other, and God does not permit one to exist without the other.

If we wholly perish, why have we been surrounded by so much of grandeur? Why are we attended by the stars, the sun, the earth? Why these constellations and these innumerable worlds far off in space? Are suns and systems to continue for all time, and man — the grandest conception of the Divine mind — to run his little race of forty, fifty, sixty years, and then disappear to return no more? Is this God's plan? If beyond the grave there is only nothingness — if after death man is only insensible dust — we make a mistake in honoring the dead. If this be so, we need build no tombs here, for why should we raise monuments to that which does not exist? But the skeptic says science fails to furnish evidence that there is life after death. Well, science has also signally failed to show how it happens that we live at all. Still, we do live. That we live a generation or an hour is as much a miracle as if we exist throughout the eternities. On the other hand science does not teach annihilation. Indeed, it disproves it. It demonstrates that all substance, gross or ethereal, is indestructible. Do we not know that reproduction is a law, absolute and eternal; that nothing in nature is barren; that there is not "a blade of grass that withers, nor an ugly weed flung away to die and rot," but reproduces something? Is it true that every living thing in the universe has its resurrection but man?

> "Can it be?
> Matter immortal! and shall spirit die?
> Above the nobler, shall less noble rise?
> Shall man alone, from whom all else revives,
> No resurrection know? Shall man alone,
> Imperial man! be sown on barren ground,
> Less privileged than the grain on which he feeds?"

The soul revolts at the thought of annihilation. Addison puts these words in the mouth of Cato:

> "Why shrinks the soul
> Back on herself, and startles at destruction?
> 'Tis the divinity that stirs within us;
> 'Tis heaven itself that points out an hereafter,
> And intimates eternity to man."

The profoundest depths of our being respond to this faith in eternal life; and the nearer we approach the grave, the stronger and brighter is the hope of immortality. Let us abide in this faith until the end. It is taught in our religion, and is the faith in which our fathers died. It is a belief that beckons us forward and upward, inspires us with high resolves and noble impulses. It will cheer us in life, and be our solace in the hour of death. It will give our lives, at all times and in every struggle, a heavenward side.

I am now done. It seemed to me fit, in this presence and on this occasion, that I should speak a word for that faith that lightens up the very gloom of the tomb. Let the stones that may be put here be not monuments of pride, or ambition, or sorrow, but of a people's faith in an overruling God and an immortal life beyond the grave.

ADDRESS OF REV. B. F. FOSTER.

Brethren of the Mystic Tie:
　　Ladies and Gentlemen:

The pleasing duty has been assigned me of saying a few words upon this interesting occasion, in behalf of the Independent Order of Odd Fellows; and in doing so I shall no doubt occupy ground in common with kindred fraternities whose representatives are here assembled. Laboring, as we are, for the good of humanity in many of its phases of sickness and suffering, it is fitting that we are permitted to meet upon a day consecrated to freedom, and join in the ceremonial of setting apart a hallowed spot as the last resting place of kindred and friends. That such organizations are necessary as society is at present constituted, but few will question. Everywhere we see the elements of antagonism at work. In church and state, in the conventional and social circles of every-day life — wherever we turned our attention, we find man arrayed against his fellow man — each acting upon the principle that this life is a mere field for the promotion of selfish and sordid ends. In the religious world, even, what a conflict of opinion — how bitter the animosities engendered at times, merely in consequence of a difference in matters of faith and church government — all striving for the same great end, yet indulging in a spirit but illy comporting with the genius and spirit Christianity! So in the political world, the utmost rancor and hatred is not unfrequently produced in consequence of a difference of opinion upon matters of state policy and political economy. Churches, at times, have been broken up or rendered powerless in their warfare with the opposing powers of evil, by these antagonisms in political life. The business world, too, has had its trials in this respect. In the din and bustle of a noisesome world, where men jostle each other in the crowd — in the mart of industry; in the halls of legislation; throughout every avenue of human life, men lose sight of the great doctrines of the divine Fatherhood of God, and brotherhood of man — doctrines which underlie the superstructure of Odd Fellowship and all kindred associations. Hence that golden rule of "doing unto others as you would have others do unto you," is lost sight of, and the precept but little regarded.

Nor has this spirit of antagonism been confined to the present age of the world. It has run through all the centuries of the past; and in the long procession of ages, from the dawn of creation up to the present hour, the principle of isolation and selfishness has characterized man's history with man. And no one who will consider for a moment the present aspect and condition of the world, as we find it illustrated in the various departments referred to, will question the fact that there is need of some institution or association that will breathe

DEDICATION CEREMONIES. 61

peace upon the troubled waters of society — that will harmonize in some small degree, at least, these discordant elements, and restore the moral equilibrium that has been violated.

It is refreshing to the true philanthropist and lover of his race, to know that the true design of life is fast becoming appreciated — that men are no longer content with the selfish, money-making and money-getting spirit of the age — but are stretching out their arms to raise and elevate human character, to relieve distress, and alleviate many of the woes of suffering humanity. And while I am proud of the organization to which I belong, and believe it to be an important agent in doing good, I am not blind to the fact that kindred orders are also entitled to the just meed of praise for the part they are taking in the great drama of regenerating and benefiting mankind.

Odd Fellowship, whether taken as a whole, or in fragmentary parts, is a system that commends itself to all lovers of their race and well-wishers of mankind. Through all its gradations, we are led step by step, to unfoldings that are sublime and beautiful, and that call forth the admiration of the studious and well-disciplined Odd Fellow.

The tyro in our order, as he enters its threshhold, is deeply impressed with the significance of those grand truths enunciated by Paul on Mars Hill, when he proclaimed the doctrines of the Divine Fatherhood and brotherhood of man. In the very alphabet of Odd Fellowship he learns a great secret, and that is a knowledge of the forces with which to gain the victory over *self*, *passion*, and all obstacles that hinder the progress of the soul in those virtues that should adorn human life in all its phases, from the cradle to the grave.

In passing through the various degrees of the subordinate lodge, he is constantly discovering new and hitherto hidden beauties, presenting to his mind grander conceptions of the great author of human existence, of the end, aim and design of his being—while within his reach are placed those instrumentalities in the use of which he is enabled to contribute his mite in lessening sorrow and in mitigating the woes and ills of life. Here he receives his first charge, "to visit the sick, relieve the distressed, to bury the dead, and educate the orphan"— a charge which finds an exemplification in his intercourse with the world. Every lesson taught in the lodge room is a lesson of love, breathing forth upon humanity the richest benedictions of sympathy and benevolence. Hence the true Odd Fellow goes out into the world with his mind thoroughly imbued with his capabilities for good, and his whole life becomes a consecration to the best interests of mankind.

Here, too, he learns the lesson of mortality— a lesson deeply impressed upon the mind by the solemn ceremonials through which he must necessarily pass. He learns that mortality is the allotment of all human nature. The insatiate acher, Death, speeds his unerring darts, and man in the pride of his strength or the humility of his weakness, is the ill-fated victim. The inexorable fiat was in the beginning established, "Dust thou art, and unto dust shalt thou return." There is no Rubicon that presents a momentary barrier to his ruthless and devastating progress. His scepter is unlimited, even over all ages and conditions of life. From the rising of the king of day to his rest, waves the wand of death, and potentate and peasant, youth and age, bow before it.

These reminders of our mortality are ever before us, calling in the mind from the ltttle narrow circle of terrestrial investigations, and encouraging therein deep and holy contemplation, thus humbling human pride, leveling all titles and classifications, and making man feel his weakness and dependence upon a Higher Power.

I would that I could dwell at greater length upon the lessons and teachings of the subordinate lodge; but time admonishes me that I cannot. Hence, I must pass on to another branch of my subject. Having once entered within our mystic temple, he finds among its watchwords, "*progress, advance, onward, upward*"—that there is no standstill point, where he may sit down and fold his arms, contented in the thought that the eldorado for which he sighed has been gained. He must needs pass on in the journey so auspiciously begun, until he reaches the door of the tent of the representatives of the ancient patriarchs, whose hospitality is ever open to the stranger and pilgrim of earth. And this brings me to notice briefly the Encampment branch of our Order.

To become a patriarch should be the ambition

of every Odd Fellow. While in the popular or representative branch of Odd Fellowship there is much to claim our attention and win our regard — much everyway worthy of our devotion and zeal in advancing its interests — we should, nevertheless, press on toward the mark of the prize of our high calling, in order that we may obtain a full knowledge of the intrinsic excellencies of our beloved Order.

In the Patriarchal branch of our Order we find the practical exemplification of the primary truths taught in the subordinate lodge — a full illustration of the grand thought of Paul, when he declared that " God had made of one blood all nations of men to dwell on the face of the earth." That however widely sundered by locality the nations of the earth may be, there is a common bond of union, that, if accepted, will unite all hearts. That no matter of what nationality or clime a person may be, who seeks admission at the door of our tent, if he brings the acceptable offering of a pure and devoted love for mankind, he will be ever welcome. In the beautiful and eloquent language of another, " The Esquimaux from the eternal snows of Labrador, and the Brahmin from the jungles of Hindostan, the polished Athenian from the midst of the glories of the Grecian art, and the rude savage from the pathless forest — the Roman knight, from the ranks above which swoops the victorious eagle, and the fierce barbarian from the wilds of Parthia, the sons of Abraham and the priests and worshippers of Isis, the Catholic and the

Prostestant, the millionaire and the beggar — these all may unite in relieving the woes and distresses of earth!"

Thus broad and universal is the dominion of Odd Fellowship as illustrated by the sublime degrees of the Patriarchal branch of our Order. In its Alpha and Omega, it is a fitting sequel to the work of the subordinate lodge. Every patriarch in his journey through this wilderness world, feels the need there is of rest. He is frequently tossed to and fro upon the angry seas of passion and discord — his pathway at times is narrow and dangerous — enemies would fain assail him from without as well as from within; but against all these elements of antagonism he is more than equal, if he heed well the lessons imparted in this higher school of Odd Fellowship. While the greatest degree of charity is taught with reference to our treatment of those who are recognized as patriarchs, the alien and stranger are not forgotten. If he fails to discover in the initiatory work the great lesson of charity and toleration, and would still remain isolated and selfish in his feelings, regarding his own party and sect the peculiar favorites of heaven's regard, the veil is at once removed as he enters this inner temple, and stands face to face with the men of every clime and nationality! "Faith, Hope and Charity," what a triune of graces and virtues are here linked together. He sees with an unclouded and undimmed vision, the elements of strife and discord disappearing like the mists before the brightening sun. If never before, he now realises the truth that all are brethren, regardless of party ties or sectarian barriers. That however widely men may differ in opinions upon questions of national policy or church government — they are all forgotten in the hour of human woe and suffering. What an ennobling spectacle does Odd Fellowship thus present — a common bond of union for men wholly unlike in every other respect. And if for no other reason, I would cling to it on the ground of its tendency to unite men of opposite and even antagonistic natures.

And it is a relief to turn away from the shadows of the past, and even from the present, where party strife, discord and wrong still linger, and contemplate the dawn of that brigher day in the future, when all these elements of antagonism shall pass away — when wars shall cease, and violence shall no more be heard in the land. When the poet's vision shall be fully realized:

"I saw in a dream sublime,
The balance in the hand of Time;
O'er East and West its beam impended;
And day, with all its hours of light,
Was slowly sinking out of sight,
While opposite the scale of night
Silently with the stars ascended.
  I saw with its celestial keys,
Its chords of air, its jets of fire,
The Samain's great Æolian lyre
Rising through all its seven-fold bars,
From earth unto the fixed stars.
And through the dewy atmosphere,
Not only could I see but hear

Its wondrous and harmonious strings,
In sweet vibration sphere by sphere,
Onward to wider and vaster rings,
Where chanting through his band of Mars,
Majestic, mournful Saturn goes,
And down the sunless realms of space,
Reverberates the thunder of his base!
    Begirt with many a blazing star,
Stood the giant Algebar!
Orion, hunter of the beast,
His sword hung gleaming by his side,
And on his arm, the lion's hide,
Scattered across the midnight air,
The golden radiance of its hair!
    The moon was paled, but not faint;
And beautiful as some fair saint,
Serenely moving on her way,
In hours of trial and dismay.
Thus moving on in silent pace,
And triumph in her sweet pale face,
She reached the station of Orion!
Aghast he stood, in strange alarm,
And suddenly from his outstretched arm,
Down fell the red skin of the lion
In the river at his feet.
    His mighty club no longer beat
The forehead of the bull;
But he reeled as of yore,
Beside the sea,
When blinded by Ænopian,
He sought the blacksmith at his forge,
And climbing up the mountain gorge
Fixed his blank eyes upon the sun.
Then through the silence overhead,
The trumpet of the angel said,
Forever and forevermore,
The reign of violence is o'er;
And like an instrument that flings

> Its music on another's strings,
> The trumpet of the angel cast
> Upon the heavenly lyre its blast,
> And on and on, from sphere to sphere,
> Re-echoed down the burning chords,
> Forever and forevermore,
> The reign of violence is o'er!"

As we look to the future by the aid of those lights of human progress which are constantly illuming our pathway, we can behold that "better time coming," gleaming brightly in the distance! That time when wrong shall be no more — when the brotherhood of the race shall be universally acknowledged and appreciated. That time we may not expect to come like a sunden burst of sunlight in a midnight sky! But if Odd Fellows are true to themselves — true to the interests of the Order, they can accomplish much in ushering in this age of millennial glory!

Aye, like some mighty undercurrent, the principles of Odd Fellowship will flow on, deepening and widening as they go beneath the surface of society, leaping up here and there in fountains and sparkling rills, until at last they shall appear undisguised and flood the whole earth! Welcome to that happy period! Eden's beauty and abundance shall be seen again; and the Father shall bless His children with His presence, and lift upon them the light of His countenance, and walk with them as in the early time. "Then shall the wolf dwell with the lamb, and the leopard lie down with the kid, and the calf, and the young lion, and the fatling together, and a little child shall lead them!"

ADDRESS BY REV. A. J. LUELLAN.

Companions and Brethren,
  Ladies and Gentlemen:

Love or charity is the noblest characteristic of humanity. It is that principle of divine origin which assimilates man to his maker, and which gave him dominion over all the earth. When in full fruition it exerts a virtuous control over every other sentiment of the soul; imparts to life the highest and purest pleasures, and inspires a steadfast hope of future bliss. To this ruling principle we can readily trace the most excellent acquirements of man. By its kindly sway those endearing relations which exist among members of the human family are cemented and preserved. Under its genial powers men are impelled to the exercise of every virtue. It is that great principle of attraction which sustains and harmonizes the moral universe. But the past eloquently admonishes us that this sublime sentiment, though regarded as inherent, has not a secure abode in the human heart. From various causes which flesh is heir to, its powers are often, alas, too often, blighted, and with it despondently droops all the better attributes of man. To encourage this heaven-born principle, and to give it perpetuity and vigor in every heart, is one of the ruling objects of Freemasonry.

Faith, Hope and Charity are vividly illustrated in our institution, and forcibly commended to the attention of every brother, but the chief of these is Charity. It is the chief good — the Alpha and Omega — the crown and cap stone of our moral Masonic edifice, being the most essential to the noblest traits and true dignity of humanity. Who, without it, can hope to enter heaven? None but those who inherit this boon from above can expect to hear those beautiful tidings from our Savior's life, as a passport for eternal joy: "For I was an hungered, and ye gave me meat; I was thirsty, and ye gave me drink; I was a stranger, and ye took me in; naked, and ye clothed me; I was sick, and ye visited me; I was in prison, and ye came unto me." Charity speaks to the poor in a still small voice while it secretly ministers to their wants. It goes without ostentation or the hope of reward to the habitations of woe, misery and cankering want, and not only mingles with their sympathy, sighs and tears, but with bounteous hands bestows more substantial relief. It goes silent as the starry dews where the arrowy winds of winter pierce the thin-clad orphan and chill the homeless widow's heart, and anon their features, pale with want and suffering, become radiant with joy and comfort. It takes the victim of the storm and restores him to a safe haven, and bids him repose in peace. It lifts the ship-wrecked mariner from the engulfing wave, and warms his stiffening form to life. It seeks the crushed and bruised by the wayside, pours oil into their wounds, and bids them go on their way re-

DEDICATION CEREMONIES. 71

joicing. It visits the chamber of the sick and the cell of the imprisoned, and there imparts faith, hope and comfort. All this and more, much more than pen can describe or eloquence express, hath charity, the genius of Masonry, the heart and spirit of our institution, performed.

Masonry proclaims to her votaries that no act can stamp more true nobility and exalted excellence upon the sons and daughters of Adam, than to impart relief and comfort to those who are truly needy; and that charity is not an impulsive throb, but a holy, and with the virtuous, an abiding sentiment, most in harmony with heaven.

One thousand and eleven years before the Star of Bethlehem shone upon the wise men of the East, our institution was permanently established and dedicated to the only true and living God. Its existence, in every essential, was commenced with the erection of the first Jewish temple, under Solomon. We learn from history that that magnificent structure was situated on Mount Moriah, near the spot where Abraham's altar stood. In its construction were engaged three grand masters, the chief of whom was Solomon, King of Israel, aided by Hiram, King of Tyre, and Hiram Abif. There were also employed three thousand three hundred master masons, eighty thousand fellow-crafts, thirty thousand assistants, under Adoniram, and seventy thousand entered apprentices. It contained 1,453 columns and 2,906 pilasters. The walls were of white marble, and so skillfully put together as to present the appearance of one solid body. The timbers were of olive, cedar and fir, from the forests of Lebanon. The nails and roof were of gold.

During the seven years occupied in its erection, the sound of ax or hammer was not heard, and so much did heaven favor the great achievement of art, genius and wisdom, that the progress of the work was not once interrupted by rain or storm. The sun steadily and approvingly smiled upon their labors, and at night, only, did the kindly refreshing showers fall, soothing their repose and slumbers. This stupendous edifice, forming the admiration and wonder of all subsequent generations, was commenced and completed under the benignant sway of Freemasonry. And thus were peace, harmony and good-will preserved among the workmen, and temperance, morality and knowledge inculcated. Thus early, at least, commenced Speculative Masonry in conferring real blessings on mankind.

Under this system it was found that men of every nation, tribe and kindred; of every sect, party and denomination, could assemble and be united in bonds of fraternal love, and with commendable emulation practice pure benevolence, strict honesty, impartial justice, and all those golden rules which are so necessary to the happy existence of a moral and social being. We behold in it a system which has stood the test of centuries. From that remote period in antiquity, from the days of Hiram, the widow's son, Freemasonry has ever been the same. She has witnessed the sad havoc of

Time—the mutability of all things earthly. She has beheld nations, kingdoms and empires, once the pride and glory of the world, arrogating immortal duration and renown, at length crumble in their onward career, and finally disappear amid the wreck of ages. She saw classic Greece and the city of the Cæsars rise to proud pre-eminence, lofty in eloquence, sublime in song, and profound in wisdom, commanding admiration and inspiring dread from all the powers of the earth. Generations passed away, and she again beheld them paralyzed by ignorance, superstition and tyranny, yielding to the unsatiable decay of time. Through this long succession of years, amid these changing and dissolving scenes of other systems and of nations, Masonry stood firm, steadfast and invulnerable, ever ameliorating the woes and miseries of man, ever abounding in acts of charity and universal benevolence. Yet, with all her purity and beauty, she has not escaped the shafts of implacable, bitter, malignant foes. The pen of falsehood, black and putrid; the tongues of slander, most foul and venomous; aye, and the weapon of murder, in fiendish hands, have been used and concentrated against her, in the vain, delusive hope of destroying her temple and extinguishing the fire from her sanctuary.

In every period of her existence, in every land and in every clime; yes, and must it be said, even in free, enlightened America, the iron grasp of persecution and direful oppression, clasped by knaves, bigots and political tyrants, has been fastened upon her very vitals. But as well might they attempt to restrain the free breath of heaven, as well strive to seize the immortal soul and hurl it into oblivion, and as fruitless would their efforts prove. Wherever ignorance and despotism have dared to trample upon the dearest rights of man, our institution, unappreciated and unheard, has been assailed, proscribed and condemned, and our brethren constrained to break, in impassioned agony, the deep, damp silence of a dungeon's gloom. Even the rack of fiendish torture has been rendered hideous in diabolical efforts to extort the secrets of our order. The scaffold, too, has reeked with the blood and groaned with the sacrifice of our devoted brethren. The power of government, and the still greater power of a distorting, mercenary press, have been united in desperate efforts to crush her fair proportions and towering, earth-extending form. Years of thick darkness threw heavy clouds around her, threatening, in a voice of thunder, her eternal doom; but she gloriously conquered every storm, and the fire upon her sacred altar, though often obscured, continues to shed its devotional effulgence. Justice, innocence and truth have been bitterly assailed by the base, ignorant, designing minions of despotism; hence, with them, it is no wonder that the victims of persecution appealed in vain to the history of Freemasonry for a refutation of the infamous charges with which the public ear was poisoned.

But it is indeed strange that under our glorious and enlightened Republic, such an institution can not escape the bitter and despotic scourge of persecution, especially when the fact is so clearly demonstrated, not to our fraternity alone, but to the world, that Masonry never suffereth the slightest connection with politics; keeps untrammeled and aloof from all party associations or conflicts; enjoins strict obedience and support to the government, and an implicit, prompt observance to its laws. Yet, passing strange as it may seem, it is, alas! too true, that even in this land of freedom, Freemasonry could not escape the fiery ordeal of a bitter, blighting persecution; such an ordeal as we have, as ever, triumphantly endured. It was a storm of truly terrific and surpassing violence; but unlike those of former times, our fraternity was, by the supremacy of the law, protected from the terrors of the rack, the faggot and the scaffold. Yet in the organization of a strong anti-Masonic political party, their oppressive and tyrannous outrages were none the less cruel and vindictive. Who of you, my brethren, have not seen the heartless and ambitious politician seeking to gain the suffrages of a free people, and thus climb with polluted hands to eminence and power, by hurling his vile machinations and slanderous words against our institution, whose principles were too pure for his personal life, and which but too severely exposed his rottenness and reproved his sins? The popular will for a time, over sensitive and yielding, like autumnal leaves to the passing breeze, became at once excited at the reports of unheard of crimes which were attributed to Masonry. So great became the tempest of excitement, so tornado-like the convulsions of the public mind, that our brethren were constrained to rest in passive, meek and unresisting silence. So dark was the cloud on Mount Moriah, that the operations of the craft were for a time suspended, and their harps were hung upon the willows of "Babylon," and they wept in silence; wept over the blind, deluded frenzy of their enemies, who refused to see the purity or inhale the benevolent spirit of Masonry.

> "Truth crushed to earth will rise again—
> The eternal years of God are her's;
> But error, wounded, writhes with pain,
> And dies amid her worshippers."

Never was poetry more truthfully applied, and have you not, my brethren, witnessed its verification? Is there here a Mason, true and faithful, having lingered with me upon our past tribulations, who can now behold our prosperous condition and flattering prospects, and not feel his eyes illuminated with a brighter luster and his heart bound with happier emotions? Honest men have at last dispelled passion and courted the return of reason. Many have studied the history and deeply reflected upon the character and designs of our time-honored institution, and now behold it abounding with great moral beauties and blessings to mankind. We again see the light in the East, shining with renewed and renewing brightness, and the clear bow of promise spans the horizon of Masonry. She has put on her beautiful garments, and by the development of her sacred mission is now proceeding, with

DEDICATION CEREMONIES. 77

fresher vigor and increased glory, in the path of public opinion.

The rule of our faith and the guide of our practice remains as unchanged, bright and inviting as in our palmiest days, and the "all seeing Eye" is still watching over us and extending around us its guarding care. But even now, and perhaps in this assembly, there may be some who feel inimical to Freemasonry. And why? I answer, and that too, without the fear of successful contradiction, that it is only because they are ignorant, wholly ignorant of our leading principles and ruling objects; and without stopping to inform themselves, regardless of evidence, and without a glimmering of proof, suffered the old hue and cry of denunciation to fill them with a deep and settled prejudice. In all candor, in the name of truth, we ask what other cause can be assigned for their hatred? What is there in the genius and spirit — what even in the forms and ceremonies of Masonry, to which an honest, upright man can consistently object? Not, surely, to the precepts and works of Masonry. Then would he complain of heaven's just requirements, for they are made obligatory upon us by God's holy word, and are held in veneration by all truly good and pious men. It is possible the old and nearly worn out hobby of secrecy bewilders the mind of some one person as an insuperable objection to Masonry. To such I will simply say that we really have our secrets—secrets worth knowing, yes, and worth keeping; secrets which we love as dearly as life, and which we cling to more closely and value more sacredly than you can the apple of your eye. Say you the possession and retention of these secrets is a crime? If you do, then truly are all men guilty, for what man is there among you, or what lady of my fair and innocent auditory, who has not closely garnered and snugly locked within the bosom's core, secrets, perhaps of an endearing nature, which the terrors and treasures of this world cannot extort? I verily believe there stands not upon this globe a rational being whose breast is not the safe repository of secrets, unimportant, doubtless, to the world, but to the retainer most precious.

Man is made up of secrets. He is a secret to himself and all save God. The sky above and the earth beneath, his being, his actions and his passions are all alike inexplicable. Who can explain this operation of the various scenes, and divulge the connecting agency between mind and matter; or who expound the source and power of electricity in the animal and inanimate universe? Surely heaven and earth abound in secrets. On every page of the great book of nature mystery is written with an iron pen. Behold it in the eternal stars which look down upon the mysterious changes of our fitful earth! See it in the summer breeze which steals so gently in its balmly visitation as to scarely disturb the silken veil that adorns the brow of beauty; and lo! in a moment the brave old oak, the dense forest, and the most enduring monuments of human architecture are wrested from their firm foundations, and swept be-

DEDICATION CEREMONIES. 79

fore this mystic breeze, like chaff, into destruction. We hear the sounds thereof, and can trace its gloomy desolating track, but cannot tell whence it cometh or whither it goeth.

Let those who charge secrecy upon us as a crime, beware lest they, also, criminate the God of heaven. In His word and in His works how numerous are the secrets which the science or wisdom of man never can penetrate. And His ways, are they not mysterious and past finding out? And His abode, is it not the center of unfathomable mystery? As Masons we believe that whatever God does is right; and as He draws the veil of secrecy over many of His noblest works, we can but feel justified in concealing from the world some good things pertaining to our mystic brotherhood. If made public our secrets would be of use to no one, but now they are invaluable to the fraternity in enabling us to know one another by night as well as by day, and to perform those duties which brother owes to brother, and which are due from friend to friend. I would say to this audience that there are no secrets in the principles of Freemasonry. They are all made public and may be found in Masonic books and magazines, and we only crave for them the scrutiny of an enlightened world. The constitutions and by-laws of our Order are freely offered to all who can and desire to read them. Our dedication and installment of officers are in the invited presence of the public. We only have, like the Senate of the United States and all other legislative bodies, our secret sessions, and these, no doubt, our Order will cling to as long as time shall last. Others object to our institution because men can be found claiming to be Masons who are profane, intemperate and reckless. That there are such men "'tis true, and pity 'tis 'tis true," but can they consistently condemn Freemasonry for the bad conduct of some of its members? As well condemn our Republican form of government because bad, dishonest men claim to be Americans. As well banish religion from the land because a few base hypocrites become members of the church, bend their knees before the holy altar, and with polluted lips partake of the symbolic body and blood of Christ. As well attempt to dethrone Jehovah, and hurl high heaven into chaos, because the arch fiend and his angels were once arrayed in glory around the beatific throne. As the angels of heaven wept upon the occasion of their fall, as the faithful pastor of his church weeps whenever any of his flock go astray, so do all good Masons lament when a brother departs from the path of moral or Masonic rectitude. Deep in the mire of infidelity and ignorance must the man be who would attribute the immoral conduct of a church member to the Christian religion; equally erroneous and unjust would be the act of imputing to the principles of Masonry any deviation of her members from their moral duties. Both institutions have the same luminary for their guide and advocate, the same cardinal virtue. There is nothing in Masonry that can be construed as incongruous to the religion of our Redeemer.

Still Masonry makes no pretentions to the great plan of redemption; usurps not the capacity of preparing the soul for a permanent abode in the realms of bliss, without the interposition of the Divine Spirit, but reposes on the broad and fundamental doctrines of Christianity. Though not a religious institution, and promulgating no theological distinctions or preferences, it is undeniably founded upon the purest and best maxims of holy writ, and has proven an efficient hand-maiden, an important auxiliary to her younger though superior and nobler sister, Christianity.

None can properly become Masons but those who believe in the existence of a God and lead an upright, moral life. The first object that greets a Mason's eye, on entering the lodge-room, is the Holy Bible, that inestimable gift of God to man, the great light and leading star of our Order, the guide of our life, and the exhaustless fountain of intelligence, founded upon the eternal rock and reared by the immutable truths of God's holy work. Think it not strange that our institution should exhibit so stupendous and harmonious a fabric of majestic and lovely proportions. Wonder not that it is crowned with universal piety, and that its capacious portals are gladly unfolded to the worthy follower of every genuine religion, upon the broad, undiscriminating platform of equality. Thus constituted, Masonry justly claims to concentrate in one great body the just tenets and approved ethics upon which all good and virtuous men of every religious and political faith may safely stand. Within her temple the discordant elements of the world do not enter. It is a retreat too sacred to be convulsed and disturbed by partisan strife, collisions and differences, which are so unfortunately rife among our fellow men when the ties of brotherhood do not prevail. There the care-worn and weary, the heart o'er burdened by wrong, oppression and deceit — from a cold and selfish world, may find serene and sweet contentment. It is the temple of refuge from sordid, corroding care; an asylum in which the spirit is refreshed by the radiant light of peace, and under the benign influence of brotherly love, relief and truth, is inspired with purer and better, loftier and wiser emotions. It is there we learn the precious mementoes of the past and the eloquent admonitions of the future. There soul mingles with soul in kindred fellowship, and it is there we study the sublime principles of our common union; we there bow before the common altar in fervent devotion and thanksgiving, and learn our ceaseless dependence on Omnipotence.

RULES CONCERNING INTERMENTS.

1. The Sexton, or superintendent of interments, resides with his family at or near the Cemetery, and will see that suitable persons are in attendance at any interment.

2. No grave will be opened without a permit from the President, Secretary or Treasurer.

3. In each case of burial, a statement giving the name, place of nativity, residence, age, disease of the person, occupation, also whether married or unmarried, must be handed to the Secretary, Treasurer or President, that an accurate registry of the same may be made.

4. The size of the coffin, (on top,) or if case, the size of the case, should be particularly mentioned; and when interments are to be made in private lots, the location of the grave in the lot should also be stated.

5. The charge for opening and closing a grave will be as follows: For all persons over twelve years of age, $5.00; for all persons twelve years of age, and under, $3.00; in case of re-interment, $3.00. These prices include the sodding of the grave, etc. Competent persons will be in the employ of the Association to exhume and superintend the removal of bodies to the Cemetery.

6. No permit will be granted or grave opened without the payment of charges.

7. The price of a certificate, or deed of lot ownership, is 50 cents; for each transfer of same, 50 cents.

8. No person will be permitted to use the lot he or she has purchased, or transfer the same, until fully paid for.

9. For receiving each corpse into the public vault, $3.00. After the first week, $1.00 per week will be charged for three months, and at the expiration of that time the body will be buried in a public lot, unless further extension of time is asked for and obtained by the friends of the deceased, and charges are paid in advance. The above charges must be paid in advance: the first before the corpse is received, the balance weekly in advance.

10. The above last named fees must be paid to the sexton at the Cemetery, and credit given by him shall be at his own risk, as his returns must correspond with the permits.

BY-LAWS.

SECTION 1. The President shall be selected from the members of the Board of Control, and shall preside at all meetings of the Board, and shall call meetings of the Board whenever he may deem it necessary, or when requested to do so by any one member of the Board.

SEC. 2. The duties of the Secretary shall at all times be subject to the Board of Control, and he shall be elected or appointed by them. He shall keep the minutes of the Board and all the books, records and accounts of the Association. He shall pay over forthwith all moneys he may collect to the Treasurer. He shall render quarterly statements of the finances and the affairs of the organization, and also a general statement of the year, to be exhibited at the annual meetings of the Board of Control, and cause notices to be published of all meetings of the lot owners whenever required to do so by the Board of Control.

SEC. 3. The Treasurer shall be elected or appointed by the Board of Control. He shall receive all the funds of the organization and deposit the same to its credit in such bank or banks as may be designated by the Board of Control, and shall disburse the same upon the order of the President. He shall make a quarterly account of the state of the finances to the Board of Control. He shall give bond in such sum as may be required by the Board of Control for the faithful performance of his duties and the faithful application of all funds that may come into his hands as such Treasurer.

SEC. 4. The Secretary and Treasurer shall hold their offices for three years, unless sooner relieved by the Board of Control, (the first ones elected shall hold only one year,) and both offices may be held by the same person, and all other agents of the organization shall be appointed and hold their offices during the pleasure of the Board of Control.

SEC. 5. The stated meetings of the Board of Control shall be the first Monday in each month, at such times and places as the Board may direct.

SEC. 6. The meeting of the lot owners for the election of one of the two members they are entitled to of the Board of Control, shall be on the first Monday in June, 1881, and on the same time each year thereafter, that the Town Board or City Council does not elect their one member of said Board.

SEC. 7. All resolutions offered for adoption shall be reduced to writing, and the yeas and nays shall be recorded on the demand of any member.

SEC. 8. Each lot owner shall be entitled to one vote for every twenty-five dollars that he has actually paid. Should the owner's lot cost less than twenty-five dollars, he shall have one vote if actually paid for, which may be cast in person or by proxy.

SEC. 9. These By-Laws may be repealed, altered or amended by a majority of the Board, after such repeal, alteration or amendment shall have been proposed and entered on the minutes of a previous meeting.

RULES AND REGULATIONS.

1. The proprietor of a lot will be entitled to a ticket of admission into the Cemetery, with a vehicle, under the following regulations, the violation of which, or loan of a ticket, involves a forfeiture of the privilege. No vehicle or person on foot will be admitted unless accompanied by the proprietor of a lot or a member of his household, with his ticket, or presenting a special ticket of admission obtained at the office of the Cemetery.

2. Children will not be admitted unless accompanied by their parents or persons having them specially in charge.

3. Schools or other large assemblies will not be admitted unless under the charge of some responsible person.

4. No vehicle will be allowed to pass through the grounds faster than a walk.

5. Driving on the paths will not be allowed, nor walking on the grass.

6. No person having refreshments of any kind will be permitted within the grounds.

7. Smoking will not be allowed within the enclosure.

8. Dogs will not be admitted.

9. Any person entering or leaving the grounds in any other way than through the gate will be fined five dollars.

10. Persons having baskets, or like articles, must leave them with the Sexton unless he consents for them to pass.

11. No horse may be left by the driver within the grounds not fastened to a post or unattended.

12. All persons are prohibited from pulling flowers, either wild or cultivated, or breaking any plant or shrub.

13. All persons are prohibited from writing upon, defacing or injuring any monument or structure in or belonging to the Cemetery.

14. Any person disturbing the good order or quiet of the place by noise or other improper conduct, or who shall violate any of the foregoing rules, shall be compelled, instantly, to leave the grounds.

15. The Sexton is charged to prohibit the entrance of all improper characters, as well as those who, though having a ticket, may be known to have, at any time, wilfully transgressed the regulations of the Cemetery.

16. The gates are open for entrance at sunrise, and are closed (except for egress) at sunset, when the roads are good.

17. It shall be the duty of undertakers to see that the proper permit has been obtained before going to the Cemetery.

18. Persons accompanying funerals are strictly forbidden to walk over other persons' lots or graves, and will be subject to a fine for doing so.

19. Drivers of all kinds of vehicles will be fined five to ten dollars or more, according to the

RULES AND REGULATIONS. 89

amount of injury, for driving over borders or boundary stones of lots.

20. None but metallic coffins shall be admitted into the public vault.

21. No person with a gun will be permitted on the grounds.

22. The Board of Control shall, from time to time, fix a scale of prices, according to the location of such lots as they may see fit to offer for sale. For the present the prices shall be 10, 15 and 20 cents per square foot, according to the location and situation of lots, this being the lowest possible price that any well regulated cemetery can sell lots for, and only about one-half the price charged by some cemeteries.

23. No vehicle or person on horseback will be permitted to pass through the grounds faster than a walk. Visitors are reminded that these grounds are sacredly devoted to the interment of the dead, and a strict observance of the decorum which should characterize such a place will be required of all. The keepers of the gates are authorized and directed to remove all who violate these rules and regulations, or commit trespasses.

24. Trespassers are liable to criminal prosecution and heavy fines. The provisions and penalties of the law will be strictly enforced in all cases of wanton injury.

25. All persons are prohibited from discharging fire arms within the Fountain Park Cemetery grounds, or over or across them. The Sexton and all persons acting under him shall have full power

as police officers to carry these regulations into effect. The rule in regard to fire arms does not apply to burials with military honors.

RULES AND REGULATIONS FOR PROPRIETORS OF LOTS.

All interments on lots shall be restricted to the members of the family and relatives thereof, except special permission to the contrary be obtained in writing from the President. No transfer or assignment of any lot, or of any interest therein, will be valid without the consent, in writing, of the Secretary endorsed upon such transfer or assignment. If any monument, tombstone, vault, or any structure whatever, or any inscription, be placed in or upon any lot, which shall be determined by the Board of Control for the time being to be offensive or improper, the Board of Control shall have the right, and it shall be their duty, to enter upon such lot and remove the said offensive or improper object or objects; provided, however, that if said structure or improvement shall have been made with the consent of the Board of Control for the time being, the same shall not thereafter be removed, except with the consent of the owner thereof. It shall be the duty of the Board of Control from time to time to lay out such avenues or walks and drives, and improve such other additional lots and sections and avenues as may be necessary, and to make such rules and regulations for the government of the ground as they may deem requisite and proper to secure and promote the general objects of the donation. The proprietors of lots, and their families, shall be allowed access to the grounds at all times, observing the rules which are or may be adopted for the regulation of visitors. The location of monuments shall be determined by the Sexton, according to the directions of the Board of Control; but in this as in all other cases, all differences of opinion between the sexton and the lot owners, and all other differences from whatever source, must be referred to and settled by the Board of Control. This clause is not intended to interfere with the tastes of any individual in regard to the style of their improvements, but to secure harmonious uniformity and keep away from the grounds what might mar the beauty of the Cemetery. It is desirable that all contracts for excavations and for laying the foundations for monuments should be undertaken by the Sexton, acting in the name of the Board of Control. Still, lot owners will not be forbidden to employ other workmen, provided the latter be under the control of the Sexton, and conform themselves to the regulations of the Cemetery. They shall not leave material on the grounds any longer than is absolutely necessary. They shall remove immediately any rubbish that may remain after the completion of the work, and put it in such a place as shall be assigned by the Sexton. They shall clear the ground, and place it in the same state in which they found it. In case they fail to comply with the above immediately, the same shall be done by the Sexton at the expense of the lot owner. Workmen

RULES AND REGULATIONS.

who shall fail in complying with these rules shall not be permitted to work again in the Cemetery, and whoever shall have employed them shall be responsible for all damages done to adjoining lots. The same will be required from those who erect monuments. The Sexton will always do the work, or have it done, at current prices, as the intention is not to make money but to guard against injury to the Cemetery. No tree growing within a lot shall be cut down without the consent of the Sexton, and no rubbish shall be left on the grounds or thrown into the avenues or alleys. The Board of Control shall have the right to remove anything which would destroy the good appearance of the place. Whenever, in the opinion of the Sexton, it shall be proper to remove trees or shrubs from a lot, notice shall be given in person or by letter to the lot owner, and should the latter refuse to consent the matter will be referred to the Board of Control, who shall decide upon the propriety of such removal. Unless six hours notice be given the Sexton, between the hours of six in the morning and six in the evening, that a grave is needed, he shall not be held responsible for the non-preparation of the grave.

Rules and Regulations to be Observed on the Park Grounds of Fountain Park Cemetery.

The park portion of the grounds of the Fountain Park Cemetery includes the low grounds of the tract extending the whole length of the same from north to south, lying between Salt Creek, the Cincinnati, Richmond & Fort Wayne Railroad, on the west, to the west side of the elevated grounds east, which grounds are accurately delineated and described on the map drawn by Benjamin Grove, Esq., cemetery engineer, of Louisville, Kentucky. This park will be open for visitors during all suitable weather, from sunrise to sunset. All vehicles and persons on horseback will be admitted at the main entrance gate to the Cemetery. No person or persons will be allowed to move their horses up or down, or across on the roads of the avenues of said park faster than a trot, nor will they be allowed to drive on the grass, nor permitted under any circumstances to leave their horse or horses unhitched or unattended. No horse shall be hitched to any tree or shrub, or other property or thing belonging to the Association, except posts placed for hitching purposes. Persons violating the provisions of this rule or in anywise injuring or defacing any property belonging to the organization, will be prosecuted to the extent of the law, and be required to leave the grounds immediately. Any person of improper character, or any person with a dog or gun, found on the park, will be ejected therefrom; any person making a noise or using profane or indecent language, who will not desist therefrom when requested so to do, will be ejected from the grounds. No children, unless under the protection of some adult person, will be allowed to remain on the park grounds. Any one caught climbing on the trees, shrubs, or injuring the flowers, wild or cultivated, or running or walking on the grass, (except at times when permission is given to run or walk on the grass;) or writing, marking or defacing, or otherwise impairing, injuring, or destroying any of the property of every kind and description, belonging to the said Fountain Park Cemetery, will be prosecuted to the utmost extent of the law. No person will be permitted to fire a gun, or pistol, or revolver, on any portion of the grounds or into or across the same. The Sexton and all persons acting under him, shall have full police authority and power to carry these regulations into effect, and is hereby required to arrest, on sight, all persons who violate any of the above provisions.

RULES CONCERNING IMPROVEMENTS.

It shall be the duty of the proprietor of each lot to place, and keep in repair, permanent landmarks of the boundaries of their respective lots. They shall be of cut stone or marble, set firmly in the ground at least eighteen inches, and shall be six inches square, of octagonal form at the top, and not be exposed more than three inches above the top of the ground. To insure the proper regulation of the grounds the grade of all lots will be determined by the Board of Control. All workmen employed in the construction of vaults, erection of monuments, etc., must be subject to the direction and control of the Board of Control, and any workman failing to conform to this regulation will not be permitted afterward to work in the grounds. To protect the grounds and specially improved lots from injury, all excavations and masonry for vaults and monuments will be made by the organization at the expense of the owner. Foundations for monuments must be built of solid masonry, and of sufficient depth to secure solid foundation, and must not appear above the regular established grade of the lots.

Wooden or other kind of inclosures around lots or graves, or setter boards designating graves, will not be allowed, only for a short time. No slab will be allowed unless placed in a horizontal position, and no head or foot-stones will be permitted exceeding two feet in height above ground, unless put in a cut-stone base, with stone foundation sufficiently deep to secure stability; provided that no head or foot-stone shall exceed five feet in height, and shall be one-inch in thickness for every foot in height, unless by special permission of the Board of Control. No vault shall be erected wholly or in part above ground, without permission of the Board of Control, and all such must be furnished with shelves having divisions allowing interments to be separately made and perpetually sealed, so as to prevent the escape of unpleasant effluvia. Such portions as are above ground must be faced with cut-stone, granite or marble. No officer or agent of the Cemetery shall be interested, directly or indirectly, in any business connected with the building of vaults or the erection of monuments. The Board of Control has no wish to interfere with the tastes of individuals in regard to the style of their improvements, and yet in justice to the interests of the whole, they reserve to themselves the right of preventing or removing any erections which they shall consider injurious to the immediate locality or prejudicial to the general good appearance of the grounds; and, also, removing or pruning any trees or shrubbery which may obstruct or mar the effect of the scenery, or may otherwise prove injurious, unsightly and detrimental.

It will be perceived from the provisions of the donation that as all the receipts derived from the

RULES CONCERNING IMPROVEMENTS.

sale of lots or otherwise must be expended in the improvement, preservation and beautifying of the grounds, no speculative interests can conflict with the wishes of lot owners respecting its management. That as all the resources will be thus appropriated either immediately or ultimately, in the formation of a fund, the interest of which shall be appropriated as required, we think we will have ample means for the perpetual embellishment and preservation of the grounds. That as the ground is exempt from public taxes and from liability for debt, and is sold in lots and burial places which are not subject to assessment or annual charges, the proprietors can never be forcibly deprived of their ground.

The price of lots has been fixed as low as they can be sold to accomplish these ends. It is very desirable that in the purchase of lots it should be done with a view of future wants, and we have never known any one to purchase too much. That purchasers of lots may acquire not only the privilege of burial, but, also, the fee simple of the ground which they purchase, no person shall have the use of or title to a lot until the same is paid for. No improvements shall be allowed on lots until they are paid for.

THE SEXTON AND HIS DUTIES.

The Sexton shall reside in the house erected for the purpose, on the Cemetery grounds, when the same is finished. He shall be present at every interment, and shall have the general direction and control, under the Board of Control, of the improvement of the premises. He shall keep a map of the Cemetery, its avenues, walks and lots, with the numbers thereof, and shall cause the boundaries of the lots, avenues and walks to be preserved. He shall see that the regulations of the Board for the preservation of the lots and property, and the observance of decorum, are strictly enforced. He shall have charge of all the property of the organization on the Cemetery and Park grounds, and on the first day of January of each year furnish the Secretary with a full and accurate inventory thereof. He shall report monthly to the Secretary the names of the workmen employed, the amount of wages due each, and all other expenses which have accrued during the month, and of all sales made by him of any property. He shall devote all his time to the interests of the organization, and for his services he shall receive such compensation as shall be agreed upon. He shall make no interment, removal, or deposit a body in the receiving vault without a permit from the Secretary. Neither the Sexton nor any other person employed in the Cemetery shall receive any perquisite for any work whatsoever connected with it, or with his duties therein, his salary or allowance being considered in full payment thereof. He shall neither sell or exchange any of the property of the Association without written authority from the President. He shall perform such other duties as the Board of Control shall require of him.

ORDINANCE No. 47.

An ordinance for the regulation of the Fountain Park Cemetery of Winchester, Indiana, defining violations and prescribing penalties therefor, and authorizing the execution of deeds.

Be it ordained by the Board of Trustees of the Town of Winchester, Indiana:

SEC. 1. That it shall be unlawful for any person or persons to ride or drive a horse or horses faster than a walk in the Cemetery grounds proper, or faster than a trot in the park grounds of the Fountain Park Cemetery; or to drive or ride on the lots, grass or corner-stones of lots; or to bring or use refreshments in said Cemetery; or to bring or allow dogs under their control, to be on said Cemetery grounds; or to leave horses unhitched or unattended on any part of said grounds, or to hitch a horse or horses inside of said grounds except the posts provided for that purpose; or to refuse to leave the grounds when ordered so to do by any officer of said town or Cemetery, or by the Sexton or any of his assistants, for the violation of the rules and regulations of said Cemetery; or to injure by writing on or otherwise defacing any monument, tombstone or other property of said Cemetery; or to use vulgar or profane language on the grounds of said Cemetery; or being found intoxicated or disturbing the order and quiet of the place; or to pluck or pick flowers, either wild or cultivated, in said Cemetery; or to injure any shrub, tree or plant; or to fire a gun or pistol in, over or through any part of said Cemetery, except on the occasion of burials with military honors; or for being found anywhere on said premises with a gun except as above provided; or for any lewd or indecent female, or for any male who associates with such lewd women to be loitering about in said Cemetery; or for any tramp or vagrant to be loafing about in said Cemetery; or for any lot owner to fail or refuse to comply with any of the rules and regulations of the Board of Control of said Cemetery. Such person or persons who shall violate any of the above requirements or provisions, shall, upon conviction thereof, be fined in any sum not less than five nor more than ten dollars.

SEC. 2. Any persons who, in making any improvements to their lots, shall fail or refuse to clean away or remove the dirt or debris caused by said improvements, to any point designated by the Sexton of said Cemetery, and leave the general surface of the ground as they found it, within a reasonable time after the commencement of the work, shall be notified by the Sexton of said Cemetery, and if not complied with within a reasonable time, said person shall be fined five dollars for each day said debris or trash shall be allowed to remain after said notice, and that it shall be the duty of the Sexton remove said obstruction at the expense of the person or lot owner who makes it.

SEC. 3. All the proceeds for fines, forfeitures or penalties, that may be derived on account of the violation of this ordinance, shall accrue and be paid into the said Fountain Park Cemetery fund for the use and benefit of said Cemetery.

SEC. 4. The Board of Control shall authorize the making of deeds to purchasers of lots, or fractions of lots, when the same is paid for, signed by their President, and attested by their Secretary, with their official seal attached.

SEC. 5. It is hereby declared that an emergency exists for the immediate taking effect of this ordinance; the same shall be in force from and after its passage.

Passed July 16th, 1880.

SAMUEL D. FOX, President.

W. P. NEEDHAM, Clerk.

www.ingramcontent.com/pod-product-compliance
Lightning Source LLC
Chambersburg PA
CBHW031412160426
43196CB00007B/987